SOCIALISM

Emile B. Ader

PROFESSOR OF POLITICAL SCIENCE
MIDWESTERN UNIVERSITY
WICHITA FALLS, TEXAS

BARRON'S EDUCATIONAL SERIES, INC.

Woodbury, New York

CONTENTS

Selected Writings

Popular interest in socialism and scholarly study of this ideology are not novel. Even ruling out the earliest utopian writers, who were the "socialists" of their days, for at least two centuries Europeans—and, later, Americans—have shown a serious concern for theories and programs designed to remodel society along socialist lines. This concern expressed itself in a volume of writing and commentary by both the proponents and opponents of socialist beliefs. Thus the contemporary student is not faced with any dearth of material on the subject.

Today's Americans, while not confronted with a direct challenge to their socio-economic system by a potent socialist party within their midst, are sufficiently aware of socialist tenets and trends as to maintain an intermittent interest in socialism's modern status. It is to assist in satisfying this interest that this modest study is produced.

The key to an adequate understanding of current socialist thought and action lies in an appreciation of its origins and the diversity of its developments. It has several roots and its branches are numerous, and any comprehension of socialism must begin with this realization. Only when an attempt is made to recognize the devious evolution of socialist doctrine—influenced by time, location, and circumstance—can a true picture of modern socialism emerge. I have tried, therefore, to give the reader some insight into the content and ramifications of contemporary socialist thought by taking him along the broad avenues and narrow winding paths over which socialism traveled, and to exemplify its multifaceted nature by examining briefly its similarities and differences as it exists in England, France, and the United States.

In addition, this work essays some realistic generalizations about socialism and attempts to weigh its potential and actual advantages and disadvantages as a theory and a practical program. The principle that brevity is most conducive to reader interest has been followed throughout.

Short quotations from socialist thinkers, critics, and spokesmen for and against the "welfare state" are appended to enhance the narrative. At the end of each chapter there are study questions and project suggestions for those who wish to pursue further consideration of its contents.

I wish to express my appreciation to the administration of the University of Tulsa for a research grant which assisted me in the collection of data and to my colleagues, Dr. W. V. Holloway and Dr. William A. Settle, Jr., whose generous cooperation contributed to the successful conclusion of this endeavor. Thanks are also due to Mrs. Freda Disch and Mrs. Leta Nunn who typed the manuscript and to the editors of Barron's Educational Series, Inc. for their careful and constructive work. The responsibility for the statement of facts, the interpretations made, and the conclusions drawn is, of course, my own.

Emile B. Ader

CHAPTER 1

CLEARING THE AIR

It is not unusual in this day of "ism-itis" to hear discussions of such concepts as liberalism, conservatism, communism, republicanism, fascism, and socialism in which the mere mention of a particular "ism" seems to be accepted by both the speaker and the listener as communicating the total theoretical and practical content of the ideology or movement in question. While popular discussion of items of current interest is desirable in a democratic society, and while there may be some educational value in generalizing about subjects whose intricacies make generalization hazardous, it should be recognized that a thorough knowledge and exposition of one of these "isms" must include a clarification of its various facets, an appreciation of the nuances of the movement in its various national settings, and a perception of the interrelationships and contrasts of its earlier and later manifestations.

There is, moreover, the danger that a continuing reliance on "labels" to convey the meanings of complicated concepts, ideas, and systems may produce unfortunate results. An erroneous conclusion about the simplicity of the concept, idea, or system may be drawn, and the postulates of an ideology may be easily distorted through over-generalization. And, stemming from such distortion, inaccuracy, or incomplete understanding, there can evolve in a democracy a public opinion demanding a certain public policy—a policy which, if adopted, would have grown from faulty premises, and which could even be detrimental in the long run to those who demand it.

Thus, when one attempts to describe "socialism," the first problem is to determine *which* socialism. Socialism as a theory and/or a political movement has appeared in various forms in different countries over several centuries, and related concepts which have a sort of "socialist" orientation have been expressed by a number of utopian theorists as far back as Plato. Any effort, then, to outline such a multifaceted ideology should properly deal not with "socialism," but with "utopianism," "evolutionary socialism," "Marxian socialism," "syndicalism," "guild socialism," "Christian socialism," "Fabian socialism," and, perhaps, other examples of what may be embraced by the word *socialism*.

At the same time, while the demands of accuracy and precision require such a treatment, this kind of fragmented approach may cloud a recognition of the fact that the socialist movement *as a whole* exhibits certain traits which may be called the *essential characteristics* of socialism though one or another brand may not conform exactly to such a list of attributes. It is in this context that considered generalizations have a special value as long as it is understood that any particular generalization may be invalid as applied to a specific expression of socialism at a particular time in a certain locale.

Even the construction of a catalogue of general characteristics presents some difficulties in that the earliest expressions of "socialist" thought, especially in its utopian forms, vary considerably in emphasis from the later versions. Still, since the basic outlook and fervor of the early theorists had an impact on their successors, and since, to a degree, their over-all objectives were similar, an inventory of socialist characteristics should venture the inclusion of attitudes which have been modified with the passage of time and with changed circumstances.

At the risk of putting the cart before the horse, this endeavor to outline the meaning and significance of socialist thought and action will begin with a statement of general characteristics. Such a characterization, it is hoped, will provide an adeqate framework for detailing the various forms of socialism subsequently. It should permit an easy recognition of those unique qualities in each branch of the movement which contribute to the whole picture, and a quick perception of each branch's deviation from the norm.

General Characteristics

1] The first characteristic of socialist movements is *an apparent dissatisfaction with existing societies of their respective times.* Plato's outline of an "ideal" state in his *Republic* is a critical reaction to the decline of the Greek city-state and the loss of the civic virtues inherent in its political institutions. Sir Thomas More's *Utopia* in the sixteenth century was a satirical attack on the institutions of his day, and James Harrington's *Oceana* in the seventeenth century was another criticism of contemporary practices cloaked in utopian form. In the eighteenth century, re-formers like Jean-Jacques Rousseau, Gabriel Mably, and François-Noel Babeuf highlighted the political, social, and economic evils of their societies and contributed to the growing body of litera-ture with a socialist tinge. In the following century, with the advent of "modern" socialism, men like Saint-Simon, Fourier, Owen, and others found in their surroundings corruption, waste, knavery, fraud, misery, and other distresses which cried out for remedy. Surely the "orthodox" socialists of the nineteenth and twentieth centuries, whether of the Marxian or non-Marxian variety, are pointedly critical of the economic and political struc-ture of modern society. In the economic sphere, private owner-ship, the profit motive, monopolies, poor working conditions, and greed have received the special fire of socialist theorists and practitioners.

There is, then, this thread of discontent and criticism running through all the commentaries which may be considered socialist in leaning. This attitude does not, of course, mark socialists as unique. Non-socialist critics of society at any period have abounded, and constructive introspections on the part of the relatively well-satisfied members of any society have produced examinations of shortcomings not too dissimilar from those of the socialists. If this characteristic is to be thought unique, its singularity is probably to be found in the *spirit* which fostered socialist dissatisfaction.

2] A second major characteristic of socialism—though it is less striking in the movement since the middle of the nineteenth century—is *the insistence that any renovation of society to correct its frailties must be consistent with moral or religious values as interpreted by the reformers.* Such concern with morality has been phrased either as a necessity to return to traditional religious precepts as a guide to life or, where the critics have been less traditionalists, as a necessity to perceive novel and *true* moral values on which to base human existence.

Plato's model for a new society was based on the assumption that there was an "objective good," an eternal verity—ascertainable by an elite segment of the population—which should be reflected in the organization and practices of the civic community. More's utopian community incorporates the virtues of morality (in the traditional sense), honesty, simplicity, tolerance, peace, and justice. Saint-Simon, though critical of the practices and principles of traditional Christianity, urged a reformation of society consistent with the ideals of human and divine justice which would improve the condition of the poor. The Christian Socialist movement of the early and middle nineteenth century, while deeply concerned with social reform in a humanitarian sense, was equally concerned that such reform should be based on and should reflect the central themes of Christianity. And even in the mid-twentieth century, Clement Attlee could note the importance of religious concepts in the evolution of British socialism: ". . . I think that the first place in the influences that built up the Socialist movement must be given to religion."[1]

This religio-moral disposition of the socialist distinguishes him from his ideological cousin, the communist. The orthodox followers of Karl Marx subscribe more completely to an interpretation of history which minimizes or ignores such values as morality or ethics. Marxian "dialectical materialism" pictures the unfolding of history in *material* terms almost exclusively. The "dialectic"—a concept developed by G. W. F. Hegel—is a process of historical analysis which sees the march of the human race in terms of movements which, in time, produce inner contradictions resulting finally in major modification or destruction of the original movements. Thus, any historical tendency or development (a thesis) sooner or later produces an opposing tendency (an antithesis) which ultimately alters the original movement and creates a new one (a synthesis).

In Marxian terms, the whole course of historical evolution is phrased in economic terms.[2] Individual and class conflict for material gain has been the overriding motive in human existence, and the attainment of improved economic circumstances the prime goal. Socialists do not discount the significance of economic goals and motives in human endeavor, but these are not the sole concerns of individuals and groups. Communism's materialism is, for the socialist, at least coated with additional intellectual and emotional considerations.

3] Coupled with this concern for "morality" as the guideline to the reformation of society, there appears in socialist thought and action a *religious fervor and dedication*. There is not merely the exposition of an idea. There is a repetition and elaboration born of a deep conviction. There is a militancy of outlook and

---

[1] Clement R. Attlee, *The Labour Party in Perspective* (London: V. Gollancz, Ltd., 1937), p. 27.

[2] For Marx, capitalism (the thesis) produces the proletariat (the antithesis) which will eventually destroy free enterprise and replace it with communism (the synthesis).

assurance of righteousness reminiscent of the exponent of a purely religious belief. The faith of the socialist has frequently matched that of the religiously devout, as has his proselyting. And the socialist crusader has been able to make converts with his vision of temporal paradise as effectively as the religious crusader with his vision of a spiritual heaven.

4] This fervor has not exhausted itself in the creation of utopian schemes. Most of the advocates of socialism have not contented themselves with "tilting with windmills" or advocating "pie in the sky." *They have been realistic proponents of practical programs of action designed to attain feasible objectives.* Though socialist philosophy has at times been idealistic or visionary, for the most part socialist practitioners have been convinced of the attainability of their goals and have sponsored projects and programs which have transformed speculation into execution. The political activities of Babeuf, the Brook Farm experiment in the United States as a concrete expression of the ideas of Fourier, Robert Owen's ventures in factory reform and his establishment of the New Harmony community in America are typical examples of socialist practice of the late eighteenth and early nineteenth centuries. The political programs and activities of socialist parties around the world since the middle of the nineteenth century are adequate testimony to the fact that contemporary socialism is not confined to an "ivory tower" approach, though the dedication to political *action* has not brought a cessation of socialist theorizing.

5] *Socialism has, on the whole, evidenced a sincere and deep concern for man—his dignity, his worth, his rights.* It is not surprising to note this humanitarian strain in socialism in view of its moral or religious origins. Man's nobility in the eyes of God could be expected to find secular expression as a need to elevate the lowest members of society to a level commensurate with their status in the Creator's realm. Even when religious overtones were less conspicuous, the plight of man in his worldly surroundings has been a sufficient motivation to socialist concern. This humanitarian viewpoint has not always centered on man as an individual; in a number of instances man in various societal groupings has attracted socialist interest. In these cases, as exemplified by Rousseau, the emphasis in socialist plans for the reconstruction of society has been on group living in which cooperation and mutuality had higher premiums than individuality.

6] As a concomitant of this last characteristic, socialism has usually not been critical of man for his own physical or moral degradation. Instead, *man's unfortunate state—the perniciousness and immorality of the established order—is held to be the result of corrupt institutions.* Owen's comment that the mill workers he managed at New Lanark had been "surrounded by bad conditions, and these bad conditions had powerfully acted upon them to misform their character and conduct" [3] is exemplary of an almost universal socialist contention that it is not people who are bad but institutions.

There may be in this assessment a certain amount of self-delusion on the part of socialists that people, individually or in the mass, are victims of circumstances over which they have no control, and, therefore, they should not be blamed for their condition or their vices but helped. There is no escaping the fact that the institutions of a society must result from the actions or inactions of its members, and to separate people from institutions is something of a fiction. Even the apathy and lethargy of the populace at large which may permit a special molding of institutions along particular lines by small segments of the society must be counted a contribution by omission to the evolution of that society's organization and mores. On the other hand, not to warp the socialist exposition from its true context, those with whom the socialists have been most concerned—the laboring masses, the economically underprivileged—had generally been born into a society whose institutions they had no voice in shaping and little chance of changing. Socialist criticism, then, was directed at those systems of society which kept the largest

[3] *The Life of Robert Owen, by himself* (New York: Alfred A. Knopf, Inc., 1920), p. 78.

proportion of its members practically in bondage and at those members of society held responsible for the perpetuation of the systems.

7] *Socialism is primarily an economic doctrine.* Regardless of the characteristics previously noted—the humanitarianism, the religious origins, the idealism—the focal point of the socialist attack on the existing order is its economic organization. And the prime socialist recommendations for society's renovation relate to economic reorientation and reorganization. From Plato to the present this element of socialist dogma stands out. It may be joined in a total plan by considerations of morals, ethics, and politics, but such considerations merely provide the environmental framework in which the major job of economic change is to be accomplished. This characteristic is, naturally, particularly noticeable in contemporary versions of socialism. The modern socialist, like the communist, makes many aspects of capitalism his prime targets. Inequities of income distribution, the profit motive, monopolies, acquisitiveness, the condition of the working class, and other expressions of the "free enterprise" economic system—at one stage of its development or another—receive scathing denunciations. And the remedies proposed are, of course, likewise economic in nature, with the improvement of the economic status of the masses being the goal sought.

The core of remedial action is the *replacement of private ownership and operation of the essential means of production and distribution of goods with collective or governmental ownership and democratic management.* Various private businesses are to be transformed into public enterprises, owned by the people (the government), and operated for the general good by representatives of the public. This process of "socialization" or "nationalization" of industries and other elements of the economy will, it is argued, eliminate the evils which flourished under capitalism.

8] *Modern socialism is essentially a product of the industrial revolution and the "factory system" which resulted from it.* While the industrial revolution and mass production have given an impetus to a rising living standard for all, originally—and to an extent even today—they created conditions upon which socialist movements could thrive. The poor working conditions which frequently accompanied the rise of industry, the long hours of employment, the low wage rates, the dangerous circumstances attendant to many jobs were soon the subjects of socialist attention. The callousness displayed by some entrepreneurs toward their employees was a spur to socialist criticism on humanitarian grounds. The mad scramble for greater profits and its by-product of unconcern for the human element in the economic process ran contrary to socialism's humane philosophy. The vast disparities in income distribution which appeared quickly as the system unfolded, the enormous gulf which developed between the great wealth of the few and the poverty of the many were sure to inflame socialist sensibilities. The eventual rise of slums which spoke so eloquently not only of the miserable economic situation of their inhabitants but of their total social and moral misfortune added another element for which capitalism could be criticized and held responsible. The periodic breakdowns of industrial capitalism—the protracted periods of depression—further emphasized for socialists the lack of economic security for workers and the "erroneous" assumptions about the advantages of free enterprise. And the persistence of such faults, the economic and political opposition to remedial efforts, served as a rallying point for the socialist reformers. The continuation of such conditions was unthinkable to the socialists on both economic and benevolent grounds. Socialist criticism culminated in practical plans for reform. Adherents were sought and gained. The longer reform was in coming the greater the socialist zeal grew as did socialist strength. And the achievement of limited reforms did not deter the setting of new objectives so long as the general status of workers remained inadequate in socialist eyes.

9] As socialism expanded its influence in modern society and theory gave way to the preparation of programs of practical action, the economic concerns of the socialists had to be placed within a pragmatic context of politics. Which best way to achieve the ends of socialism? The socialist answer to this question has generally been *a belief in gradualism.* Evolution rather than revolution has been the watchword. The necessity of "educating" the whole of society to the evils which exist in order to construct a springboard to an improved social order has been recognized by the socialist as the first step in the journey to sound progress. Adequate organization for a concerted political effort was recognized as taking time. Even convincing the workers themselves of the potentialities for self-improvement was not something which could be done rapidly. Faced with the existence of institutions and attitudes which were antagonistic to their objectives, socialists have realized that permanent modification of society to conform to their ideals—without risking the chaos inherent in the violent upheaval advocated by communists—would take time and hard work.

10] Along with this belief in gradualism socialists have generally committed themselves to the corollary principle of *acting within the constitutional and legal framework of the society they wished to reform.* While noting the fact that democratic techniques might be inapplicable where dictatorial totalitarianism prevailed, *socialists have normally urged the use of democratic processes for the attainment of their goals* in countries where such processes were available.

The rejection of revolution and the adherence to democratic evolution as the prime means to the desired end seems to be predicated on two principles. First there is the assumption that democracy of and by itself is an educational and uplifting stimulus for the working classes. It teaches the virtues of patience, tolerance, cooperation, self-reliance, and persistence in effort—virtues which are deemed essential to the erection and operation of a socialized society. Revolution, on the other hand, as Harold Laski pointed out, unleashes passions and emotions which are antithetical to those required for cooperative, harmonious living. Hate, conflict, and clash are not easily transformed into communal serenity.

In an even more practical sense, democracy is favored over revolution as being the most likely—if not the only—method for securing socialist aims. As Karl Kautsky pointed out: ". . . a Socialist Party which is unable . . . to obtain the support of a majority of the people in a democracy will find it even more impossible to obtain such a majority by the use of armed force or the general strike. For in the latter instance the weapons at the disposal of the opponents of socialism will prove even more effective than under the form of democratic struggle." [4] In other words, if, as the Marxists claim, the capitalists are so well entrenched in their positions in society, a test of violence is more likely to favor the capitalists than is a contest of ballots. The socialist movement may even be set back irretrievably by a crushing defeat in overt hostilities, whereas an electoral loss in a democratic setting still has an educational value which can be utilized for the future.

Thus, democracy is not only a tool, but a tool with a dual utility. It is inherently instructional and morally creative, and simultaneously it offers the best operational approach to the successful transformation of an economic system in a hostile atmosphere. To be sure, socialists do not reject *completely* the possible necessity for some resort to violence, but, as a generalization, dedication to democratic methods is a basic socialist tenet.

In everyday terms use of the democratic process implies the formation of socialist societies, political parties, and producer and consumer cooperatives; socialist propagandizing, particularly in trade unions; the running of socialist candidates for public office; the election of a sufficient number of such candidates as to constitute a legislative majority; and finally the socialization or "nationalization" of the economy by law. The extent of the socialist commitment to this democratic pattern is particularly exemplified in the British experience where the

---

[4] Karl Kautsky, *Social Democracy versus Communism* (Rand School Press, 1946) quoted in William Ebenstein, *Great Political Thinkers* (New York: Rinehart and Co., 1951), p. 737.

British Labor (socialist) party was voted in and subsequently out of office, and where the resurgent Conservatives de-nationalized some areas of economic activity previously nationalized by the Laborites. The Labor party, nevertheless, continued to fight politically according to the ground rules of Britain's parliamentary democracy.

11] Further characterizations of socialism in modern terms should be made to distinguish it from orthodox Marxism or communism. *Socialist doctrine generally does not demand the total socialization of the economy* as does the communist. *Government ownership and operation need extend only to certain segments of the economy,* though state planning might encompass much of the economic activity which remains in private hands.

Among the major items which require nationalization the socialists cite first the public utilities—heat, light, power, transportation, communication. Not only does the entire population depend so regularly on such services for them to be left in the sphere of profit-making, but they tend to be "natural monopolies," a characteristic which further enlarges the opportunity for "exploitation." In the fields of industry and commerce, such activities as banking, steel production, and the extractive businesses (petroleum, mining, etc.) would be socialized. Agriculture might or might not be nationalized, but would be at least regulated. Smaller enterprises, arts, crafts, and various areas of distribution and exchange would remain in private hands. Though this "limited" aim of socialists might not make their system any more attractive to the supporters of free enterprise than is the communist, it is a mark of differentiation.

12] Another difference between socialism and communism and an additional substantiation of socialist belief in legality is the *socialist acceptance of the idea that compensation should be paid to the owners of private property which is nationalized.* Unlike the communists who believe that property should be expropriated from "capitalist exploiters" without compensation, socialists, though they are highly critical of capitalism, still hold that private owners should be compensated commensurate with the "fair" value of the property taken. This procedure of seizure of private property for public use with just compensation is merely the exercise of the governmental power of eminent domain which exists in any society. The question of what is "just" compensation is always, of course, a debatable issue. In the socialist scheme, payment is generally made in the form of interest-bearing government bonds which may or may not equate with the owners' estimate of the worth of their property.

13] Finally, still another characteristic of the socialist movement distinguishes it from communism. Socialists, in their march toward the attainment of their objectives, *do not foresee either the establishment of a dictatorship of the proletariat or the eventual "withering away" of the political state as do the communists.* In their gradualistic and legalistic approach, the socialists see no need for the imposition of a dictatorship to root out the last vestiges of an entrenched capitalism or to provide the coercive political framework within which to establish a new system. The political processes at hand will prove adequate to their tasks.

As regards the state, the socialists do not view the state exclusively as a weapon of exploitation in the hands of the ruling capitalist clique or as an essential evil which ultimately must vanish if the millennium of harmonious living is to be reached. Rather, while the socialists concede that the institutions of the state may be used for exploitative purposes, they also argue that, with proper motivations and in proper hands, these same institutions can be tools for the amelioration of the society. The state, then, actually represents a great potential for good if appropriately utilized.

SUMMARY

These characteristics give an over-all view of a movement which has persisted, in one form or another, through the years. Though the modern variants may differ in form and emphasis from the earlier types, socialist theory and practice evince a considerable consistency in motive and objective. Socialist theorists and practitioners all seem to have been struck by similar observations of their environments and similarly stimulated to remedial action.

The end result has been a picture of an expression of dissatisfaction with the existing state of society, based initially on moral grounds, and an urge to reform that society in line with the moral convictions of the reformers. The reformers, generally speaking, have not been dreamers but have believed deeply that the remedies which they sought were practically attainable, and they concocted programs of actions consistent with this belief. For the most part, the socialist movement has concerned itself with economic reform of a type designed to improve the lot of the masses in line with socialist ideas of the dignity and worth of each human being. This humanitarian motif in socialism cannot escape notice. The modern movement gained special impetus from the economic and social by-products of the industrial revolution when economic inequities became more pronounced and the condition of labor became so impoverished. While fired with a religious zeal, the movement has been basically moderate. Gigantic, overnight modifications have been neither sought nor expected. Slow, sure progress has been the path followed. Socialists have repudiated the revolutionary tactics of their fellow collectivists, the communists, and have trusted in democratic maneuvers to reach their goals. Though sharing the communist position in opposition to capitalism, socialists have broken with communists on several additional grounds: the overemphasis on the exclusively economic interpretation of history inherent in dialectical materialism; the degree of socialization of society required for the best life; the question of compensation for nationalized property; and the matter of dictatorship and the future of the political state.

A final caution should be made that the foregoing generalizations may be overly broad, that inadequate emphasis may be given to some features and too great an emphasis to others.

Nevertheless, the following description of specific forms of socialism should substantiate the listing and indicate the special source of one or another of the characteristics.

STUDY QUESTIONS AND PROJECT SUGGESTIONS

1. To what extent can "socialism" be considered a unified and consistent philosophy or program of social renovation?
2. How can socialism's original religio-moral bent be considered as a stepping stone to its later economic objectives?
3. How are the institutions of any society developed, and to what degree do they determine the potential of the individual for self-development?
4. Outline the basic economic tenets of "modern" socialism.
5. What are the basic motives which prompt socialists to adopt democratic, legal processes for the attainment of their goals?
6. How do the essential tenets of socialism differ from those of orthodox Marxism?
7. Why is it important to be able to distinguish among various types of socialism and to recognize that "socialism" and "communism" have distinctly different characteristics?

CHAPTER 2

THE EARLY
UTOPIANS

The word *utopia* usually connotes a plane of human and material perfection which may be possible only in the imagination. It suggests a place or a system in which such ideal perfection is achieved or achievable. It implies, perhaps, a visionary outlook or a naivete unrelated to reality on the part of the proponent of utopia. On the other hand, the portrayal of a utopia may be simply a subtle technique for criticizing existing institutions instead of resorting to a bald attack on contemporary inadequacies. It may imply a sincere belief in a degree of possible perfectibility of both humans and institutions. It may set forth an ideal not as an attainable reality but as an exaggerated picture of the room for improvement in current affairs and as a spur to remedial action within practical limits. It is in these latter senses that the utopian political philosophers have made their great contributions, and it is as critics of their respective societies and prophets of particular brands of social change that they are precursors of socialism.

Plato

Probably the first major exposition of a political, social, and economic utopia is found in *The Republic*. In this work Plato mourns obliquely the passing virtues of a declining Athens by advocating a new kind of Greek city-state in which "justice"— the ultimate virtue—is created and assured. Faulty education, party strife, factionalism based on competing economic interests, defective leadership, and the ills of the citizens themselves called for a "perfecting" of the Greek democracy. The overriding spirit of Plato's ideal state is cooperation and the mutual satisfaction of needs through the voluntary efforts of the three major segments of his perfected society. Justice in this context consists in the honest performance of the duties assigned to the respective classes and the honest recognition and approbation of the contribution each makes. This implies a selflessness in all and a realization that the welfare of all is advanced by the efforts of each no matter what station in society is held.

Plato sees the necessity for three categories of citizens to perform the three functions on which the existence of the society depends. There must be farmers and artisans to provide for the physical needs of the population. There must be soldiers to protect the society. And, most important, there must be "guardians" to rule. Each group performs a specialized task for which its abilities and its training fit it best. Plato gives some recognition to the possibility of mobility among the classes but believes that this will be at a minimum. This fact, however, seemingly will not lead to psychological or economic dissatisfactions which could disrupt the society's perfection. There is an assumption here, of course, that the well-being of the state and its total population will be held to be of greater significance than that of the individual member of society and that psychic satisfaction will be derived from the individual's sense of contribution to the larger good. Plato held further that the proper educational system, including the dissemination of myths, would not only prepare each class for its special functions but would create an atmosphere which would minimize frictions between classes.

Prime attention is given in Plato's analysis to the role of the guardian class. They have the greatest responsibility because they must govern the community, and government is an art requiring great knowledge, extensive training, and rigorous discipline. The guardians or philosopher-kings, chosen because of their natural aptitudes and subjected to a prolonged education, alone possess the insights to perceive the "eternal good" and to apply it to the affairs of the state. Therefore, Plato is specially concerned with the total conditions of life for these guardians so that all their energies may be dedicated to the task of governing.

Private property "beyond the barest necessaries" is denied to the guardians—though not to the rest of the population—so that they will not pursue material wealth instead of attending to the art of ruling. "Wives are to be held in common by all," as are children, so that the attraction of the family will not compete with the guardians' loyalty to the state and so that the best offspring will be produced. The removal of these hindrances to unswerving dedication to duty is to be coupled with the most vigorous training of the mind and body over a long period of time to produce the most capable rulers.

Plato's work cannot be classified as "socialist" on several counts. Basically he is non-materialistic. He preaches class cooperation rather than class conflict. He surely sees no classless society. He indulges in no revolutionary exhortation. Nevertheless, he is in the socialist stream in his criticism of his society and his emphasis on communal living for the benefit of all. The concept of common ownership of property in the guardian class—and common possession of spouses—outstrips the similar concept in contemporary socialism. The idea of "eternal verities" as standards to be applied to the art of governing matches the socialist contention of society reformed according to moral values. And

Plato's blueprint for the ideal state parallels socialist programs for the attainment of their goals.

English Utopians

Sir Thomas More. Thomas More, lawyer, commercial agent, Member of Parliament, and Lord Chancellor, was in an excellent position to observe the social and economic ills of sixteenth century England. From these observations, and prompted by the ethical compulsions of his theological and philosophical interests, More produced his *Utopia* in 1516. His work is both a criticism of existing evils and a blueprint for social reconstruction mouthed by a mythological traveller who, like More, is a believer in natural law.

On the critical side, More sees no justice in a society which heaps rewards on the rich and makes little or no effort to improve the lot of the working classes who are the backbone of the commonwealth. Money and its pursuit appear as the root of all evil; private property is condemned as being antagonistic to just government and general prosperity. The enclosure movement, transforming farmland into sheep pasture, not only leads to a shortage of food but drives the peasant from the land. The growth of poverty gives rise to crime as a means of sustenance, and the criminal is then severely punished by the society which pushed him to criminality. The maintenance of a large standing army is also criticized by More as being likely to lead the country to war.

More's fictitious community avoids these ills of British society through a carefully conceived plan of organization and the inculcation in individuals of special virtues through education and the habit of communal living. Agriculture is the prime economic activity to which every inhabitant devotes a portion of his working time. Each worker is also trained in a trade to which he applies himself when not engaged in farming. The more onerous tasks in the society are performed by convicted felons or foreign laborers, though the latter are treated kindly. Basic needs of the community are calculated and met, but there is no striving for luxury. As basic material requirements are met or exceeded, leisure time is increased. Agricultural and manufactured products are placed in common storehouses from which each family freely secures those items necessary to satisfy minimum needs. There are no attempts to grasp more than is required for the moment, as each person is confident in a future abundance. Money is not used, and precious gems and metals are demeaned through regular homely use.

While a rather elaborate governmental structure exists, laws are few and simple. The spirit of cooperation and understanding and the happy life of virtue and simplicity are engendered more through education and the practices of daily living than through legal coercion. Private morality is emphasized as a pre-condition of public morality, and freedom of worship is guaranteed. Meals —which are taken in large groups—and leisure time are used to supplement formal training in expanding intellectual horizons. The value of knowledge and study is highlighted not only by a system of compulsory education for all but by absolving the more able from the obligation of toil so that studies may be pursued without interruption.

It is in these ways that the inhabitants of Utopia seek to promote the happiness and welfare of all. Cooperation and communalization are cornerstones of society; simple living and the virtue of honest toil are extolled; luxury is shunned and morality praised; the needs of the spirit are satisfied equally with those of the body; and the ingrained habit of conformance to the community's standards stands as the chief assurance of individual rectitude. Visionary? Perhaps. But as social criticism and a plan for reform, More's work is a prominent signpost on the road to socialism.

Sir Francis Bacon. A century after the publication of More's *Utopia* there appeared Francis Bacon's *New Atlantis,* another of the utopian works which have periodically fired man's imagination. The humanism of More's England had been supplanted by a new interest in science and experimentation, and it is not surprising, therefore, to find Bacon's scheme cast in this mold.

Bacon was considerably less concerned than was More with man's social and psychological needs and much more concerned with his physical well-being and material advancement. No rearrangement of property relations is urged; no moral revisions are required. Instead, Bacon sees the basis of man's future happiness in the proper application of science to the affairs of society. His mythical island is the epitome of such application supported by a few moral regulations which round out the context for an ample and dignified human life.

In that he fails to deal with some important aspects of the social and economic organization of his society which could account for man's distressed state, in that he chooses to mute his cry of condemnation of the unfortunate situation of the masses, and in that he grasps too readily a partial remedy as a panacea, Bacon is not really in the direct line of socialist thought. However, as he recognizes the vast potential for improvement in man's state—thus indirectly at least bemoaning his present status, and as he spotlights one avenue of approach to such improvement, Bacon lends his weight to the broad crusade for the elevation of the common man.

Other English Utopians. Britain's civil strife in the middle of the seventeenth century served to stimulate further considerations of ideal political, social, and economic arrangements in organized society. The publications emanating from this environment were not "utopian" in the sense that they erected fictional societies based on collectivist principles. Rather, they attempted to analyze the social and economic problems of British society and to recommend changes which were, to say the least, idealistic, with little hope of immediate attainment. One outspoken group which arose claiming that political reform must be supplemented with economic reorganization was the Diggers. As interpreters of natural law the Diggers argued that such law prescribed a communal right to land and subsistence and granted to the individual the privilege of sharing in the produce of the common land. Through their leading spokesman, Gerrard Winstanley, the Diggers urged the creation of a commonwealth in which the marketing of land would be prohibited and in which ownership of private property—excluding personal effects—would be limited. In this "utopia" all able-bodied persons would engage in common labor, and the production therefrom would be placed in common store from which all could draw according to need. The Diggers sought to demonstrate their beliefs through the cultivation of unenclosed land—a project which was short-lived. Though the Diggers made only a small ripple in the vast pond of social and economic reform, their words and actions indicated a sincere continuing concern with the maladies of their society and prospective cures.

Other exponents of radical reforms in seventeenth century England were Peter Chamberlen and John Bellers. Chamberlen, in *Poor Man's Advocate*, outlined the debt which the rich owed the poor and stated that the purpose of wealth creation should not be the enjoyment of the rich but the elimination of poverty. Therefore, Chamberlen proposed the nationalization of royal and church property and public exploitation of natural resources for the benefit of the poor. These opinions were later reinforced by those of Bellers who urged the establishment of cooperative colonies in which, with initial public financial underwriting, the poor could support themselves through their communal efforts.

James Harrington's *Oceana* should also be noted in any catalogue of utopian contributions to the development of socialist thought. Written primarily to suggest a sound basis for the permanent settlement of English revolutionary issues, *Oceana's* principal merit is the analysis which it gives of the interrelation of property ownership and the exercise of political power. Harrington makes clear the coincidence of land holdings and political authority and pleads, from a republican viewpoint, for a scheme of land distribution to diffuse economic and political might among the many rather than the few. He couples this with an entire program of democratic political processes—many in vogue today—modified with the principle of aristocratic leadership which combination, he believes, will provide the necessary balance to promote a stable commonwealth.

Thomas Campanella

The outstanding Italian utopian, Thomas Campanella, demonstrates in his own work the influence of Plato and More as utopian advocates. Out of a life compounded of monastic withdrawal, political conspiracy, prolonged imprisonment, and a continuing search for knowledge, Campanella produced in the 1620's his *City of the Sun* as a description of the ideal society. The structure of Campanella's work is a combination of the Platonic dialogue and More's use of the seasoned traveller describing his observations of a mythical community. Its central theme is the virtue of a society fashioned, like Plato's, by its philosopher leaders.

Unlike most later socialist advocates, Campanella is critical not only of the institutions of society but also of its "raw material," man himself. Thus his idealized state is predicated on the reformation of both man and his environment. Again the recognition of the impact of Plato's thoughts is inescapable as Campanella unfolds his plan for regulated human breeding and condemns the conventional family relationship as detracting from man's loyalty to the state. More forcefully than any of his predecessors, Campanella depicts paternal pride and desire to enhance the material position of offspring as the motive force in the amassing of private property with its disintegrating effect on the community.

To extirpate this unfortunate influence, one of the Sun City's practices is a strikingly intricate pattern of relationships in human reproduction (unrelated to individual preferences) to improve the species, and a second is the requirement that children be reared and taught in groups—outside any family circle—from the time that they are weaned.

In the educational process children are taught the virtue of toil—the more arduous being the most praiseworthy, the satisfaction of communal living, a patriotism that is adequate incentive to maximum efforts even in the absence of personal material gain, respect for magistrates, and a general attitude of moderation. Demonstration of special aptitudes in the early years leads to special training and, ultimately, to specialization of employment in the satisfaction of the society's needs.

Government is in the hands of an elected aristocracy of knowledge and learning which has the prime responsibility for ordering the affairs of the community to produce an harmonious existence. Neither wealth nor poverty is to be permitted. Every person must be satisfied in the simple wants and each must be prevented from obtaining more than a fair share.

Campanella's support of a communized society goes much further than that of most of his predecessors, particularly as regards family relations. But his concern for eugenic regulation may be evaluated as one expression of the recognition that society's reformation has to begin with its basic unit, man. Institutional revision may be only a partial or temporary answer to pressing social and ecomonic problems which can be finally solved only in man's individual moral and intellectual rejuvenation. In any case, Campanella defended the "community of women" as being natural and as contributing to the proper development of the race. It was "moral," he said, in that directed reproduction was not an expression of lust or lasciviousness but a manifestation of shrewd political calculation for society's improvement. Indiscriminate relations, he emphasized, were not permitted; only those sanctioned by the law could occur.

Campanella further defended communism as being consistent with human nature by reference to the prevalence of communized groupings in earlier history, particularly among the clergy. He also rejected the contention that communism destroys incentive as a misconception growing out of man's egoism in a culture of private property. Where the culture and education of the community emphasize labor's virtue and a fair but moderate compensation for all, he says, the community spirit will be a better incentive than monetary gain.

The French Utopians Through the Eighteenth Century

Just as English revolutionary upheaval in the seventeenth century stimulated a spate of reform writing, so, in the eighteenth, the economic and social abuses of the French monarchy and aristocracy led to the French Revolution and—along the way—to a large number of critical tracts with a socialist orientation. It is perhaps more correct to speak of most of the authors of these works as "social critics" [1] rather than utopians; but again, though the literary vehicle is not consistently the imaginary community, the suggested modifications were frequently far-fetched.

The first French utopia of consequence was the *Histoire des Sevarambes* by Denis Vairasse, published in 1675, a forerunner of the avalanche of eighteenth century criticism. The setting for the Sevarambian society was an Australian island; its guiding principles were the elimination of pride, greed, and idleness. To accomplish these purposes private property and inequality of social status are eliminated. Labor is compulsory and idleness is deemed the greatest disgrace. The people live in common dwellings wherein are stored the commodities of life which are drawn as needed. Education is stressed and molded to the ends of the society.

There is nothing particularly novel about this presentation, the influence of earlier utopians being easily seen. What significance it possesses rests in its contribution as a stimulant to the social and economic critiques which follow.

One such social critic, Jean Meslier, a comparatively unknown clergyman whose work was published posthumously, attacked

[1] See Max Beer, *The General History of Socialism and Social Struggles* (New York: Russell & Russell, 1957), Vol. II, Book 1, p. 198.

viciously not only the temporal organization of society but the organized church and religion of which he was a part, seeing them merely as instruments to keep the lower classes cowed and obedient.[2] The inversion of justice in a society where vice is rewarded with riches and virtue with poverty even leads him to question the existence of God. The material communism of the early Christian societies, he contends, was perverted for the faithful into the other-worldly communism (communion) of the spirit while the clergy—or part of it—continued to enjoy the finite benefits of communal living.

Meslier condemns private property and its spur to inequality as a violation of natural law and the source of economic discontent. Only in a return to the cooperative spirit, the common labor, and the mutual sharing ordained by the natural law, he contends in his *Testament*, can man find the way to the elimination of the evils in his community and the enrichment of his life.

The Abbé Morelly, too, saw the misconstruction of natural law as the basis of society's maladjustment. Nature, he contended, provided in man and its own resources those elements which would produce an admirable balance and the total satisfaction of human needs in organized society. However, says Morelly, the leaders of society began to misinterpret nature's laws and created various institutions and practices which upset the balance nature intended. Chief among these unsettling developments was the recognition of private property. Another was improper education, and a third was the marital relationship.

Morelly urged modification of each of these institutions, with the elimination of most private property being his chief aim. Productive goods, he says, should be owned in common. Each person should contribute his labor according to his talents and share from common stores according to his needs. Trade with other communities should be on a barter basis, and surplus storable products should be retained for times of scarcity.

---

[2] This bears, of course, a striking similarity to modern communism's description of religion as "the opiate of the people."

Gabriel Mably shared Morelly's ideas on the evil of private property and the desirability of substituting for it a system of common ownership, labor, and sharing. Recognizing, however, that such a proposition was too extreme in the face of man's rapaciousness and the opposition of entrenched interests, he contented himself with advocating more moderate reforms for his age. Property rights should be curbed, he argued, the right of inheritance restricted, and real estate and other capital holdings taxed most heavily, while workers' wages are lightly taxed. He further urged that efforts be made to equalize salaries wherever possible.

Though better known as a social contract theorist and a prophet of democracy, Jean-Jacques Rousseau, as a critic, saw the deterioration of a healthy "state of nature" and the necessity for the creation of organized society in the beginnings of private property—an insidious inequality requiring regulation. Rousseau's personal background made him only too well aware of the unfortunate state of the unpropertied, and his ideal society is a small classless one in which all members enjoy the economic fruits of communal living and the political benefits of the exercise of the "general will."

The last in this list of contributors to eighteenth-century French utopianism, François-Noel Babeuf, was as much a political activist as he was a utopian publicist—a fact for which he paid with his life on the guillotine. After a brief tenure as a land surveyor and minor government functionary Babeuf entered the revolutionary movement and inaugurated what was probably the first communist newspaper ever published. He attacked the revolutionary leaders, was arrested for his pains, then later released. He turned to the formation of an "underground" group designed to overthrow the existing regime, but the plot was discovered; he was again arrested with his comrades and finally condemned to death.

The principles which underlay Babeuf's actions would be better described as communist rather than socialist, but his insistence on equality and his willingness to accept a degree of gradualism in methodology are in the socialist vein. Nature, according to Babeuf, gave to every man an equal right in the enjoyment of all goods. Thus, private property contravened the law of nature and the community of goods which Babeuf sought. Those who had enriched themselves to the detriment of their fellow men were no better than criminals and should be dispossessed of their gains.

In his revised society Babeuf envisioned common labor as the common lot. Equality for all—even to dress—was to be the ideal. Education was to prepare children for the common life. No economic extremes would be tolerated, and the government would exercise a firm control on the people to insure equality. And to prevent further the possible accumulation of wealth, no inheritance would be permitted, property of the deceased reverting to the state.

SUMMARY

From the foregoing account the essence and impact of early utopianism can be gleaned. Though they differ in detail, all of the utopias recognize ills in existing society and specify a mythical (or more practical) remedy for such ills. Most see the institutions of society as evil; some acknowledge that the evil may be within man himself. Regardless of the point of departure in analysis and recommendation, the utopians collectively provide an interesting check list of evils and cures:

1] Private property is contrary to the law of nature.
2] Private property is the central cause of society's sickness.
3] Private property must be replaced with common ownership.
4] Common labor for all and common sharing in the fruits of such labor is the goal to be sought; both wealth and poverty must be avoided.
5] The virtue of communal living is recognized and reinforced by the habit of communal living.

6] Some leadership group (government?) must exist to direct the common effort and enforce the common good according to plan.

7] Arduous labor is a virtue.

8] Education must be utilized as a tool to produce the proper temperament for communal living and to motivate each person to exert himself to the utmost in the absence of material incentives.

9] Regulated breeding may be desirable in the interest of the society.

The step from utopianism as idea to utopianism in practice was not long in coming.

STUDY QUESTIONS AND PROJECT SUGGESTIONS

1. What advantages attach to using the "utopian" format as a means of social criticism?

2. After referring to Plato's *Republic, Statesman,* and *Laws* write a brief essay indicating the extent to which he modified his original utopian position in favor of a more practical organization of society.

3. A number of early utopians concerned themselves with the family relationship and the educational system as significant factors in determining the nature of society. Discuss each of these elements as you feel it bears on the development of any society.

4. In a brief essay defend the proposition "Private property is not contrary to natural law."

5. Summarize the major premises of early utopian writing and indicate the extent to which you believe they possess any validity in contemporary American society.

CHAPTER 3

UTOPIANISM
IN ACTION

Utopianism through the eighteenth century did not, for the most part, lead to any attempts to put enunciated ideals into practice even on an experimental scale. Utopian schemes remained in the theoretical realm. With the advent of the nineteenth century, however, the influence of their predecessors and the growing pressures for economic and social reforms led the new generation of utopians to couple theory with practice—to put their plans to the pragmatic test.

Etienne Cabet

Born during the French revolutionary period, Cabet was trained in the law, followed a career in politics and journalism, and, subsequently, exiled himself to escape punishment for criticism of the French monarch. In England, he became acquainted with the work of Sir Thomas More, which in time led him to produce his own version of a utopian society in *The Voyage to Icaria*.

The mythical Icaria is described in terms typical of the other utopians. The physical structure of the "promised land" is postulated on scientific principles *à la* Bacon. The state owns and directs the economic activities. The equality of the citizenry is reflected not only in the sharing of economic produce but in similarity of dress. Concern is shown for the marital relationship which is monogamous. Interestingly enough, there are no newspapers, and though the arts are encouraged, books must be approved by the government for publication.

For Cabet, this utopia could be realized gradually through appropriate education of the young, abetted by legislation which put a floor under wages and which taxed the rich to narrow the gulf between wealth and poverty. But he did not stop with the advocacy of such laws. Instead, Cabet believed that the way to attract converts and influence society was by demonstration. He, therefore, secured a land grant in Texas where he planned to establish his colony, but transferred his operation to Missouri in the face of yellow fever. Unfortunately for Cabet his plan was doomed to failure. Perhaps because of his own ineptitude as an organizer and leader, his followers did not create the harmonious existence for which he hoped, and internal crises finally destroyed the "utopia," though elements of the original Icarian colony persisted in the United States until 1898.

Henri de Saint-Simon

With the Comte Henri de Saint-Simon the "golden age" of French utopian socialism arrives. Saint-Simon's career as philosopher and social reformer did not begin until he was past forty, by which time he had participated in both the American and French revolutions, been imprisoned for a year because of his aristocratic background, and sampled many theoretical and practical aspects of life as a prelude to developing an all-inclusive philosophy.

While Saint-Simon's principal work was his *New Christianity,* earlier efforts gave some hint as to his basic tenets. He suggested, for example, that since the clergy had failed to incorporate scientific advances into its thinking it had forfeited its position of leadership in the intellectual realm. Further, he emphasized through a parable the preponderance of worth of French philosophers, scientists, and artists compared to French noblemen, ministers, clergy, and military leaders. This concern with the importance of science and industry and the relative unimportance of the aristocracy and clergy is manifested in Saint-Simon's later work.

Saint-Simon was one of those social critics who wished to reform society in accord with moral principles outside of the bounds of organized religion. He saw contempory religion as a misconstruction of God's primary admonition to "love one another." As this was the prime law, society's aim should be the greatest good of the greatest number—the improvement of the condition of the most numerous class, the poor. His method for accomplishing this end should not be completely unacceptable even to proponents of modern capitalism. Leadership, according to Saint-Simon, should be vested in the talented, especially in industry, and in economic activity, each person should labor according to his capacity and be rewarded in terms of his productive works. Thus, presumably, the more able, the more ingenious, the more ambitious would receive the highest awards.

However, Saint-Simon probably parts company with laissez-faire advocates when he suggests that a consistent application of this thesis requires the abolition of inheritance so that in each generation the able may rise on their own merits without facing the obstacles of competition from those of inherited wealth and strength and "noble" birth. His emphasis on the amelioration of the condition of the poor, his argument for public ownership of some industries, and his attack on organized religion also were not likely to endear him to the propertied classes.

Saint-Simon urged that revision should occur through persuasion rather than violence. He opposed idleness in either the rich or the poor and sought a society in which work would be available to and required of all. While he championed the principles of primitive Christianity, he did not recommend its asceticism. He pleaded for a cessation of war and a deemphasis on the importance of the military class. He was a delineator of class differences, but not an advocate of class conflict.

Saint-Simon's practical influence is seen particularly in the actions of his disciples headed by Barthélemy Enfantin and Saint-Amand Bazard who, for a time, shared the leadership of his followers. Publications, lectures, and organizations spread the "gospel." For a brief period there was even a communal grouping living at Menilmontant with Enfantin. The proselyting of the Saint-Simonians was not confined to France; missions of conversion were conducted as far away as Egypt. In the end, however, organized action disintegrated in the heat of internal controversy.

Charles Fourier

Born in 1772, Charles Fourier developed a much more plebian life than Saint-Simon and a considerably more mystical philosophy. He early became impressed with the waste, dishonesty, excessive competition, and monopolistic tendencies of the commercial practices of his time which eventually led him to set down his prescription for the reordering of society in accord with "God's will."

The key to successful living, according to Fourier, was the recognition of the principle of "attraction" which implied the release rather than the restraint of human passions. Man's impulses and passions impel him toward desired objects and toward united, harmonious action with other men. Though individual unrestrained passion may produce anti-social acts, passions given free play in carefully organized groups—contrary to popular opinion—will not only not be antagonistic but will conduce to the greatest harmony because of the interplay and dovetailing of the variety of desires represented in the group.

Thus, association rather than individual economic enterprise was called for. Ideally, society should be organized in phalanxes of approximately 1500 persons in which the greatest mixture of talents would be sought. Such associations would be capitalized for industrial and agricultural development. The inhabitants would be centrally housed and would use common warehouses, but Fourier did not advocate a "community of goods." Instead, his plan proposed a rather formalized distribution of produce among labor, capital, and talent in accord with the contribution each made, with the largest proportion going to those performing the most disagreeable tasks. Though labor was to be organized for each task, laborers were to "give vent to their passions of attraction" by choosing that endeavor which most pleased them and by being permitted to switch jobs every few hours if they so chose. In this manner labor was to become not a drudgery but a joy.

Fourier opposed violent change and believed that example would suffice to propagate his theories. The cooperation induced by the pleasure of passional freedom, he believed, would guarantee the satisfaction of human needs, an increased productivity, a greater efficiency in production, and a large measure of happiness. Yet the one experiment in which he participated at Versailles failed, as did the others instigated by his followers after his death. When Fourier's ideas came to America in the middle of the nineteenth century, over thirty experimental communities were established, including the famous Brook Farm in Massachusetts. All of these perished, but the concepts which they embodied left their mark on socialist thought.

Pierre Joseph Proudhon

Pierre Proudhon was born into a poor family and performed a number of menial tasks to pay for his education. He became a brilliant student, and his broadening interests and intellectual honing led him to intensive investigations of the nature of economics and government and to the publication of his conclusions on society's institutions. In some respects Proudhon seems to be simultaneously an anarchist, a revolutionary, a Marxist, a socialist, a utopian, an anti-communist, and a democrat. In the final analysis, neither he nor his followers initiated practical experiments based on his ideas, but he made an impact on socialist thinking which bore fruit in later years.

As an anarchist, Proudhon attacked government as a defender of the rich and an exploiter of the poor, as a supporter of special privilege, and as a traitor to the purpose of advancing the common good. He denied that government "by the consent of the governed" was a reality and seemed to feel that whatever virtues government possessed were outweighed by its vices. He proclaimed that revolution was inevitable and desirable—but not necessarily always violent, because the "haves" habitually are unwilling to make concessions to the "have nots" at the very moment when the many are no longer willing to bear the burden of want and oppression imposed on them by the few.

In typical collectivist fashion he attacked private property as "theft" and devised a labor theory of value which measured the worth of a commodity by the amount of labor which went into its production. Proudhon's criticism of property is not complete in that he accepts some aspects of private property as good and essential, *e.g.*, the individual farmer tilling his own soil for his own benefit. What he objects to is the perversion of the institution of property—or of the practices of division of labor and competition—into instruments of exploitation and injustice. Rents, profits, and interests he saw as such perversions. Labor was the only true productive force, because without it capital would of necessity be inactive. Yet he opposed communism which he viewed as an oppressive autocracy, restraining freedom, limiting the individual's initiative, and substituting for personal judgment the nebulous, passionless judgment of the state.

As a "democrat," Proudhon served in the French National Assembly and sought to utilize its processes to institute his plans of free association. More important, he insisted on a recognition of individual equality which contemporary proponents of democracy might be hard put to accept. He minimized inequalities of natural intelligence, and insisted that special talent and ability should not receive special compensation since even the "genius" is the product of the society which produced him—his expression of talent colored, guided, supported by the total environment in which he flourishes.

Proudhon's major remedial suggestion was utopian. He urged the organization of a national bank—capitalized from taxes on property and the salaries of bureaucrats—from which laborers could obtain the instruments of labor through loans made without interest. Commodities could be deposited with the bank and paper issued in exchange which would entitle the bearer to purchase any other commodities of similar labor value. This banking procedure would obviously have a telling effect on rents and profits as well.

Some of Proudhon's theory can be seen to be contradictory. For example, without governmental interference, equality of opportunity with the instruments of production, combined with human differences, would inevitably lead to inequities in private property. Be that as it may, his incisive analyses of some of the underlying assumptions, motives, and practices of his economic system shed much light on its fallacies and shortcomings, and the need to reform that system.

Louis Blanc

Louis Blanc, though coming from a royalist family, became an ardent champion of labor as an educator, journalist, and politician. His philosophical goal was the development of the individual personality through fraternal organization directed by the state. The prior principles of authority and individualism which had governed human behavior were both inadequate.

Authority represented too much the triumph of blind faith, autocracy, and inequality. Individualism, while exalting the individual and his rights, left him to depend too much on his own resources—mental and physical—for his own improvement, and these were too frequently incapable of providing the needed lift. Fraternity as a guiding principle preserved the individual effort and dignity of individualism but added the assistance of the individual's "family," the state. The attainment of this end was to be secured by education and legislation, not by revolution.

Blanc, like Marx, saw competition merely as a way station on the road to monopoly, and he felt that the main obstacles in the path of the workers' rise from economic and intellectual impoverishment were the absence of capital and credit. Therefore, he urged the government to establish "social workshops," financed from taxes and other revenues and equipped with sound machinery and tools, in which workers would be employed at their specialties on equal terms. After the first year the workers themselves would choose their administrators from their own number. Profits were to be allocated for 1] sharing among the workers, 2] care of the aged and infirm, 3] support for workshops in deficit, and 4] expansion of the workshop. Blanc, unlike Saint-Simon, rejected the principle of compensation according to productivity and insisted instead on rewards according to needs, thus characterizing differences in capabilities as marks of the social duties which must be borne by the more able.

Following the Revolution of 1848 Blanc had the opportunity to participate in the establishment of national workshops along the lines he had advocated. The opposition to this project was great, however, and several of the principles he believed should be incorporated were purposely omitted. In view of this environment of hostility the workshops did not last long, and Blanc did not live to see even a significant start in the direction in which he urged his society to move.

Footnote on America

The foregoing sketch of the ideas and programs of the leading nineteenth century French utopians most surely does not give an adequate impression of the impact of their thought. The dearth of practical success might be deemed an index of comparative failure of idea. But strangely enough it was in the United States—a country which has never enthusiastically espoused socialist doctrine—that the importance of this utopianism could be observed.

Men like Albert Brisbane were sufficiently moved as to study, contact, and popularize the utopians. Horace Greeley, editor of the New York *Tribune*, engaged in a lengthy editorial debate with a colleague on Fourier's principles. William Ellery Channing, Parke Godwin, Charles A. Dana, Ralph Waldo Emerson, Henry Thoreau, and others discussed at length and publicized utopian theories. George Ripley, a Unitarian minister, led the Brook Farm experiment. Other advocates established phalanxes which, though they ultimately dissolved, persisted intact for over a decade. The reasons for such failures included insufficient planning, too little capital, poor selection of participants, inadequate skills represented, or the difficulty of transferring a foreign ideology to a new environment. But failure or not, the surge of support in America among persons of influence for both the ideas and the experiments gives some recognition of the contribution of the theorists.

Robert Owen

Robert Owen was probably the greatest activist of the nineteenth century utopians. After an early apprenticeship which contributed greatly to his education Owen became associated with a Manchester cotton mill and rose rapidly to the managerial ranks. In 1800 he took over the management of a cotton mill in New Lanark, Scotland, which he had purchased with several partners. It was here that Owen's career as a social reformer began.

Owen's first steps mark him as a benevolent paternalist rather than an outright socialist, though his moral tone and the nature of his immediate objectives put him definitely in the line of socialist thought. As one who believed that it was institutions— not men—which were evil, Owen's prime goal was to provide for the workers at New Lanark the kind of environment which would be most conducive to their happiness and to the enhancement of their productive potential.

He first set out to improve sanitation and was successful in inaugurating a new regime of cleanliness in the community. He fought against drunkenness and attained a new level of sobriety in his workers. He argued for religious freedom and toleration. He established a community store where the necessities of life could be purchased by employees at far below regular retail prices. He built new schools at New Lanark for improved educational opportunities, and he instituted a program of medical benefits for his workers. He shortened the hours of work and raised the minimum age of employment. All of this was accomplished while profits rose.

Eventually, internal disagreements caused Owen to leave the mill, but the success of his experiment led him to the jousting ground of broader social problems. He embarked on a campaign of education and persuasion of his fellow manufacturers but with little success. When the end of the Napoleonic Wars caused large scale economic misery in Great Britain, Owen publicized his analysis of some of the ill effects of the industrial revolution —overproduction, lack of markets, and technological unemployment—and unfolded his utopian plan for dealing with the current problem. Colonies of 500 to 1500 workers were to be established on 1000 to 1500 acres of land with central dwellings, dining rooms, etc. and with all other facilities necessary to make them self-contained economic units. These were to be initiated either privately or publicly. Agriculture was to be the prime employment, but manufacturing on a modest scale would be practiced. This physical plant was to operate on a cooperative basis which would assure not merely a sufficiency of production but a surplus which would underwrite various welfare services. The plan did not have a wide appeal, but it led to the formation of various cooperative societies in England to foster the idea, and placed Owen in the forefront of the whole cooperative movement.

Owen's enthusiasm for the plan was such that he went to the United States to create an experimental community of this sort at New Harmony, Indiana. Unfortunately, internal dissension over principles and practices caused a dissolution of the colony in 1828 after three years of effort.

But Owen's zeal for reform did not diminish nor did his energy. On his return to England he began to agitate for a system of labor exchanges where producers could deposit goods, receiving for them labor notes equivalent to the worth of the goods in labor time. These notes could then be exchanged for other goods of like value. In 1832 such exchanges were actually opened in England but subsequently failed for various reasons. Even then Owen continued his activities as part of the trade union movement.

Robert Owen was an idealist and a utopian. Like all utopians who worked for and hoped to see their visions of a better world achieved during their lifetimes he was doomed to disappointment. His failures were many and his impact only slight on his contemporaries, but he was not without influence and his efforts were worthy. His dedication, his vigor, his tirelessness, his commitment to his cause were, irrespective of immediate results, an outstanding example of humanitarianism, selflessness, and conviction of right. His insights into man and his environment were revealing; his analysis of his country's economic system penetrating. He helped cut the path for Britain's cooperative societies and trade union movements. And, above all, he demonstrated what could be done practically for the average mill worker under the proper guidance and with the proper motives, and he showed that such advances in physical and moral well being could be accomplished without a diminution of revenue.

Later Utopians

While the grand era of "modern" utopian writings occurred in the first half of the nineteenth century, the utopian form and idea did not end there. So long as there remained evils in society there appeared those who would highlight those evils and suggest remedy through the description of a fictitious community. And so it may well be in the future.

The utopias of more recent vintage have not differed much from their predecessors in form, but, as H. G. Wells has explained, their goal may be a bit different. The early utopian writers sought not only to call attention to the waste, fraud, and misery of their times but to suggest a *permanent* panacea. They felt they had discovered those fundamental principles which, when properly applied, would provide an unchanging assurance of society's happiness and progress. Not so the moderns (excepting, of course, the "millennium" of Marx's analysis which is only partly utopian). The later utopian writers seem to have learned that change is too constant, human nature too flexible and fallible, for any proposed context of progress to be more than a moderate improvement—a foothold for further advance. Perhaps the more recent writers have been too impressed with the disillusionment of their predecessors to dare the outline of static perfection. Perhaps they are simply more astute. At any rate, utopias remain with us.

Outstanding in the new breed are Edward Bellamy's *Looking Backward*, William Dean Howells' *Traveler from Altruria*, Theodor Hertzka's *Freedland—A Social Anticipation*, William Morris' *News from Nowhere*, and H. G. Wells' *A Modern Utopia*.

Utopian Contributions

The later utopians as well as the early were uniform in their condemnation of social and economic injustice and in their calls for reformation. Though they did not in most cases formulate programs of political action as did the orthodox socialists, by idea and experiment they showed the way to a higher status for the individual burdened by the oppressions of his societal environment. In their criticisms of excessive competition, in their highlighting of some of the dangers inherent in the concept of private property, in their praise of work, in their advocacy of cooperation, and in their recognition of the role of education in effecting change the utopians provided their socialist successors with much ammunition.

STUDY QUESTIONS AND PROJECT SUGGESTIONS

1. Outline the important practical utopian experiments in the nineteenth century and indicate their significance to the socialist movement.

2. To what degree does Saint-Simon's philosophy accept or reject the beliefs of the capitalist philosophy?

3. Assess Fourier's contention that the "release" of human passions in a properly organized society will produce harmony rather than conflict.

4. Write a brief essay on the topic: "Robert Owen—the most prominent utopian experimenter."

5. Recent utopian writers have been more subjective in their proposals than their predecessors. Is the attempt to specify "absolute" principles to govern societal relations more or less constructive than utopian proposals which essay only tentative guides for improvement?

6. Has "utopianism," in theory or practice, led to concrete developments in twentieth century society? Explain.

CHAPTER 4

CHRISTIAN AND ORTHODOX SOCIALISM

We have already noted that the whole socialist movement, especially in its early stages, was overlaid with moral and/or religious convictions, but one phase of socialist development came to be particularly identified as Christian socialism. Though Christian socialism was manifest in a number of countries, its origin lay in France and its most significant expression in England in the middle of the nineteenth century.

Robert de Lamennais

Robert de Lamennais, a French Catholic priest, was the initial spokesman for Christian socialism. It was a unique socialism which he expounded in that he tended to reject the concept of state-controlled enterprise as being too restrictive of liberty, and he was unreceptive to the idea of class conflict. Lamennais' socialism did, however, recognize the need for greater equality—including economic—among the members of his society, and he conceded that the state must have a role in creating the conditions under which such equality could develop, especially in making the means of production more readily available to all. This material up-grading was not to be an end in itself so much as it was to be a means to allow all men to lead a true Christian life.

Lamennais saw the existing social and economic evils of his time as evidence that man had failed to heed God's laws and had perverted the order He created. In order to rectify this situation, not only must there be a return to the principles of early Christianity, but the Church as an institution must take an active part in the reformation of society. This reformation was to proceed on a broad front, but its focus was to be Church sponsorship of laboring associations which, through cooperative endeavor, would free the workingman from the economic bondage imposed by the highly competitive system of his times. Unhappily for Lamennais, his program, which was at first greeted warmly by high Catholic authority, became less and less attractive to the church hierarchy and never acquired the sponsorship he sought.

English Christian Socialism

The Christian socialist movement in England in the 1840's was similar in philosophy to that of Lamennais to the extent that it sought society's reformation in line with Christian principles and that it viewed such reform not principally in a material context but rather as a necessary part of the environment required for a Christian life. The whole mood of the movement seems to have reflected equally a desire for economic change and the inculcation in the workers of a recognition of the responsibilities which greater liberty and the Christian ethic imposed. The English

version of Christian socialism was of greater practical consequence, however, because of the time and circumstances in
which it originated—its affiliation with the Chartist development in England (essentially a demand for broadened democracy), and its emotional affinity for the revolutionary activity in
France in 1848 (even though Christian socialism itself was non-
violent in its approach to remedial action).

The founders and leaders of the movement were John M.
Ludlow, Frederick Maurice, Charles Kingsley, and Charles Mans-
field. These Christian socialists saw the sad state of contemporary
affairs as an abandonment of God's order and called for a return
to true Christianity. Like Saint-Simon they were critical of the
inactivity or fratricidal strife of the formal religious sects, and they
condemned the alliance between the organized church and the
wealthy as a collusion designed to keep the masses docile and
poverty stricken. They attacked the doctrines and supporters of
economic laissez-faire as failing to take into account humanity,
morality, and reason regardless of the accuracy or inaccuracy of
their "natural" economic postulates. They vehemently denounced
the sweatshops of the clothing industry and the philosophy of
greed which they represented.

The Christian socialist "program" to obliterate these ills was
less a "practical politics" movement than it was a set of convictions to be expounded through discussion, pamphleteering, education, moderate pressuring of Parliament, and limited economic
experiment. A weekly gazette, *Politics for the People,* appeared
in 1848 to rally the working masses to the cause. Kingsley's
pamphlet, *Cheap Clothes and Nasty,* raked the sweatshop system. A later weekly, *Christian Socialist,* expounded the leaders'
viewpoints, and was followed in 1852 by the *Journal of Association.* In the 1850's the Christian Socialists created several producers' cooperatives, established a Workingman's College, and
gave support to the trade union movement. In all of these activities, the central theme of practical Christianity emphasizing
brotherhood, cooperation, self-sacrifice, human dignity, and re-

sponsibility were reiterated. Evolutionary change and cooperative forms of production, distribution, and exchange appear as
the process to and nature of the new society.

As was true of other early experimenters, the English Christian
socialists failed to establish their reforms on a permanent basis.
As an influence on later socialist trends their impact cannot be
denied.

Christian Socialism in Other Countries

The concept of "Christian" socialism was, of course, not confined to England. The very nature of its precepts would lead to
the expectation that churchmen and laymen in other countries,
with or without the stimulations of French and British exponents,
would sooner or later become concerned with the social and economic conditions of the underprivileged and seek a renovation in
terms of Christianity. In Germany, Bishop Wilhelm von Ketteler,
Franz Moufang, Franz Hitze, and Adolph Kolping condemned
the inequitable distribution of capital and income and the sorry
lot of the wage earner, and they called on the church to lead
the way to transformation of economic practices. Their persistent
preachings led to the formation of workers' clubs, cooperatives,
and trade union activity. In Austria, Rudolf Meyer, Karl von
Vogelsgang, and Karl Lueger carried on the crusade for beneficial labor legislation and cooperatives, though the latter's anti-
Semitism cast a shadow on his constructive endeavors. In France,
such leaders as Albert de Mun, Armand de Melun, and René
du Pin waved the banner of Christian socialism as successors of
Lamennais. The Papacy, while not an enthusiastic sponsor
of socialism in any form, has indicated in both the nineteenth and twentieth centuries its deep concern for the
status of labor in a predominantly capitalist economy. Both the
Rerum Novarum of Leo XIII and the *Quadragesimo Anno* of
Pius XI emphasize the dignity of labor and the obligation of

entrepreneurs to use their capital for socially desirable purposes. Nor was the United States untouched by the developments. Since the latter part of the nineteenth century Christian social- ism has had numerous advocates and supporters in America, notably among Protestant clergymen. Early leaders included Josiah Strong, W. D. P. Bliss, Richard T. Ely, Washington Glad- den, and Walter Rauschenbusch. More recently, such eminent persons as Paul Tillich and Reinhold Niebhur have been affili- ated with the idea.

The various expressions of Christian socialism have not, of course, been uniform in tenet or action. In some instances the prime intent was to interest the church in the welfare of the masses. In other instances the actual, if not announced, intent was to urge the masses toward the church and thus enhance that institution's stature and authority. Initial advocates were not committed to state intervention as the panacea for economic inequity; later proponents have been more willing to make com- mon cause with orthodox socialists. In any event, Christian so- cialist propaganda has forwarded the socialist movement gen- erally and has served as a mitigating influence on the more violent and materialistic branches of socialism.

Evolutionary (Orthodox) Socialism

In 1848, not only did *The Communist Manifesto* of Marx and Engels appear, but Europe was rocked by a series of revolu- tionary disturbances instigated in large measure by the economic distress of the masses in various countries. This series of events seems to be a watershed in the history of the socialist movement marking the beginning of what might be called modern social- ism. From this point forward the river of socialist thought splits into two main branches, the one of revolutionary Marxism, the other of evolutionary socialism, the latter having several major tributaries.

Ferdinand Lassalle

The early leader of what came to be the German movement of orthodox socialism was Ferdinand Lassalle, the son of a Jewish silk merchant. Of outstanding intelligence and perspicacity, Lassalle made a brilliant record at the universities of Breslau and Berlin and became a prolific writer on a wide range of subjects. He became interested in popular revolutionary movements and was imprisoned briefly for urging armed resistance to political authorities.

As political contention in Germany heightened in the 1850's and early 1860's Lassalle, in an address before a workers' meeting in 1863, struck the spark which led to the creation of the first labor political party. Dismissing cooperative societies and credit unions advocated by Herman Schulze-Delitzsch as palliatives, he urged direct political action—peacefully and legally—for the revision of economic inequities. Labor, he said, must strike out on its own, dissociated from other groups, to attain universal, equal, and direct suffrage as a tool for reaching its goals. Nothing less would suffice. Goaded by Lassalle, the workers chose to form the Universal German Workingmen's Association as an independent political party with Lassalle as its chief.

Lassalle's economic theories were essentially Marxist. He accepted the labor theory of value and Ricardo's "iron law" that labor's wages would always remain at the minimum level necessary to maintain subsistence. He further accepted the Marxian theory of "surplus value" in the price of a commodity to which labor was entitled by its work but which was actually expropriated by the capitalists. To remedy this situation, workers must establish producers' cooperatives with credit from the state whose function it was to create the positive conditions for economic and social improvement of the laboring class. This latter view, of course, alienated Marx and his followers who saw the state exclusively as a weapon of exploitation in the hands of the ruling entrepreneurs.

Lassalle was destined to lead his group for only a year as he was killed in a duel in August 1864. At that time, membership in the Association had reached only 5000, but by 1867, when Johann Schweitzer had become president of the Association, a limited expansion of the suffrage was granted.

The Marxist opposition to Lassalle culminated in the formation, in 1869, of the Social Democratic Labor Party led by Wilhelm Liebknecht and August Bebel. While not outright revolutionists, this group was much more radical in orientation and international rather than national in outlook. Among its demands the Social Democratic Labor Party called for universal, equal, and direct suffrage; abolition of the privileges of birth and wealth; freedom of the press and of association; and limitations on hours of labor and on the use of child labor.

Leaders of both socialist parties had, by 1870, achieved membership in the North German Reichstag, but the Franco-Prussian war weakened the movement and suggested the desirability of a fusion between the two wings. This was accomplished at Gotha in 1875. The agreement reached created the Socialist Workers' party as the vehicle for future action to gain the objectives of the working classes. It recognized the international character of the labor movement, but it adopted the Lassalle position on the establishment of producers' cooperatives with state assistance. Marx was highly critical of this *détente* with the Lassalle group, and he denounced the evolutionary tactics to which the new party subscribed.

This union rejuvenated the socialist movement and increased its electoral strength and representation in the Reichstag. Reaction to this growth set in, and repressive measures were adopted by the Reichstag placing a ban on socialist meetings and the distribution of socialist literature. Though this had the effect of driving the movement underground, socialist votes continued to mount, and some moderate social reforms were instituted to placate the workers.

During the dozen years of restraint the socialist leaders argued over strategy and tactics, the revolutionaries insisting on more militant action. Finally, in 1891, when legal restrictions had been lifted, the movement reorganized at Erfurt. It adopted the name of the Social Democratic party of Germany and, while not calling for revolutionary action, adopted a program which was definitely Marxist in nature. It attacked the concentration of the means of production in the hands of the few; it decried the gulf between wealth and poverty which was constantly widened by the periodic crises of capitalist society; it insisted on the socialization of the means of production and dropped the demand for producers' cooperatives with state aid; it aligned the workers of all countries in common cause; it emphasized the necessity for political power as the means to economic reform; and it characterized the emancipation of the proletariat as the key to the emancipation of the human race from all forms of oppression and exploitation. These broad aims were accompanied by a statement of more specific objectives including universal suffrage, a people's militia in place of a standing army, equality of the sexes, progressive taxes, maximum hour laws, and various kinds of social insurance.

Eduard Bernstein and Revisionism

In the constant succession of action and reaction in the realm of idea and policy it is not surprising to find a developing antagonism to the Marxist philosophy which had become ascendant in the socialist movement. This antagonism was not, of course, directed to ends so much as it was to means. The leader of this revisionist trend was Eduard Bernstein. Born in Berlin in 1850, Bernstein worked briefly as a bank clerk after his schooling, then joined the radical movement. Exiled to Switzerland and later to Britain, he came to know Engels and the leaders of the Fabian Society, the latter obviously influencing his views on the social struggle. He returned to Germany in 1900 and proceeded with the advocacy of revisionism which he had begun earlier.

The revisionist school took issue with the doctrines of Marx at many points, though granting the partial validity of most of his contentions. To begin with, Bernstein objected to the over-emphasis laid by Marx on the economic factors in interpreting history. Conceding that Marx acknowledges the presence of other influences, Berstein nevertheless argued that insufficient stress was placed on the importance of cultural patterns, morals, and law in the life of a society. He agreed with Marx that surplus value existed as an empirical fact, demonstrating exploitation, but he denied that the concept was more than an abstraction—incapable of use in measuring the degree of exploitation of the workers, as commodity price was the product of several subjective factors—not labor value alone. Bernstein declared that Marx was in error in predicting the increasing cleavage of society into two competing classes with the elimination of the middle class in the process. Changes were occurring, he conceded, but not nearly at the rate Marx expected, and while the number of capitalists was growing, such "capitalists" had varying degrees of wealth, and the middle classes remained virile. Further, the proletariat was not being further depressed but was actually gaining politically, socially, and economically. Monopolistic combinations were observable, said Berstein, but this phenomenon also varied between industries, and in agriculture very little concentration of wealth and power had occurred at all. The economic crises of capitalism were, for Bernstein, another empirical fact, but such crises were not having the debilitating effect on the system forecast by Marx, and it was most unlikely that they would lead to a complete collapse of capitalism in the near future. Therefore, Bernstein stated, it was wrong to prescribe proletarian tactics of violent revolution and the forcible seizure of political power based on an assumption of the imminent deterioration of capitalism.

The revisionists emphasized democratic techniques and the evolutionary process embodying the principles of liberalism. In this light Bernstein advocated cooperation with rather than opposition to liberal parties on the part of socialists, and he urged the workers to prepare themselves intellectually and emotionally for the responsibilities they must shoulder under political and economic democracy. He sought a way to progress through moderation in which trade unions would play a leading role and consumer cooperatives would be much in evidence. Universal suffrage remained a prime immediate objective.

Karl Kautsky and the Marxists

Bernstein's position did not go unchallenged. Those who believed as did Marx were quick to respond to the criticism of the revisionists with their principal spokesman being Karl Kautsky. Kautsky identified himself as a revolutionary, but the revolution for which he spoke was not one of violence; rather, he advocated a revolution of idea and organization of society. In fact, though speaking in defense of Marxist principles Kautsky and his colleagues appear to be not very far from the revisionist position. Their replies to Bernstein seemed to involve matters of degree in interpretation rather than fundamental differences.

While conceding the difficulty of exact interpretation and prophecy, the Marxists reemphasized the economic factors in human history. They attached more importance than Bernstein to the theory of surplus value. They argued that continuing concentration of productive resources was the significant fact rather than the varied rate of such concentration in different industries. They noted that middle class incomes did not guarantee the perpetuation of the middle class as such. They suggested that crises would sufficiently weaken capitalism that a socialist revolution could be accomplished without capitalism's utter collapse. They saw, despite Bernstein's evidence to the contrary, an increase in class antagonism. And they began to speculate further on the nature of the forthcoming socialist state.

In this latter regard, Kautsky depicts several important features of contemporary evolutionary socialism. He foresaw, for example, that most of agriculture and many small industries would remain in private hands. He suggested that compensation should be given for private property which was socialized. And he pointed out that material incentives would be adequately replaced by the incentive of the simple custom of work—especially with labor made more attractive, and by the self-imposed discipline of the proletariat.

Tenets of Orthodox Socialism

The parties and programs to which Lassalle, Bernstein, and others made such an important early contribution may be justly considered the kernel of orthodox or evolutionary socialist thought. In many countries, including the United States, precepts and political activities only slightly dissimilar from those of the German movement grew. Though there may have been differences in emphasis in the various nations and among the various leaders, into the twentieth century the tenets of orthodox socialism remain relatively constant.

There is, first of all, the universal condemnation of the capitalist economy with its private property, profit motive, monopolistic tendencies, concentration of wealth in the hands of the few, and periodic crises. There is the demand for public ownership and operation of the primary means of production as one way to a more equitable distribution of income. There is some acceptance of the Marxian analysis of history pointing to the ultimate decline of capitalism through its inability to cope with its inherent crises. There is an insistence that democratic and gradualistic processes be relied on to accomplish the aims of socialism, and that trade unions and cooperatives play a major role in the transition. There is the striving for limited practical goals in terms of suffrage and the conditions of employment. There is the belief that compensation must be offered for nationalized property. And, finally, there is the contention that incentives of habit, discipline, service, and self-satisfaction can replace the monetary one of capitalism.

STUDY QUESTIONS AND PROJECT SUGGESTIONS

1. In what particulars did Christian socialism differ from orthodox socialism?

2. Discuss briefly the topic: "The institutionalized church was interested in Christian socialism primarily as a means of increasing church membership and influence."

3. Outline the basic tenets of the Social Democratic party of Germany as procalimed at Erfurt in 1891.

4. On what ideological points did the revisionists take issue with the Marxists?

5. Write a brief essay on the theme: "Karl Kautsky—revolutionist or evolutionist?"

6. Summarize the essential beliefs of the orthodox socialists.

CHAPTER 5

FABIAN SOCIALISM

While socialism of one form or another was evolving on the European continent, based on the efforts of the Chartists, men like Robert Owen, and a variety of British writers, social progress was occurring in Great Britain. Some slight advances had been made in broadening the suffrage; improvements had been made by law in the conditions of employment in mills and factories; the trade union and cooperative movements were gaining adherents and slowly proving their worth. These developments did not, however, undermine the socialist drive. Instead, they added new vigor to socialist persuasion of the need for further reform, and they tended to shape the path which British socialism would follow.

Fabian socialism became the distinct contribution of the English to modern socialism, but it was preceded in organization by the Social Democratic Federation—a Marxist-oriented group created in 1881 under the leadership of Henry Hyndman. By 1884 the Federation had formulated a long list of demands including the collectivization of the means of production, distribution, and exchange. In that same year, however, some of its leaders deserted to form a separate organization, thus depriving the parent group of some of its vitality. The Federation continued in existence, nonetheless, until World War I.

The Fabians, opposing the Marxist viewpoint almost completely but being unquestionably thoroughgoing socialists, came into being in January, 1884. They designated themselves the Fabian Society in honor of the Roman general Fabius whose patience and strategy of delay in fighting Hannibal were so successful. The roster of members grew to include many eminent and influential persons such as Sidney and Beatrice Webb, Sidney Olivier, Graham Wallas, Annie Besant, Edward Pease, Percival Chubb, William Clarke, George Bernard Shaw, H. G. Wells, Ramsay Macdonald, Keir Hardie, Harold Laski, and G. D. H. Cole. The Fabians disagreed thoroughly with the Marxist emphasis on violent revolution to accomplish socialist objectives and insisted that the achievement of the socialist society could come only from peaceful, gradual, democratic tactics. In this vein the members of the Society dedicated themselves to pamphleteering, political party activity, the preparation of legislative measures, securing membership in legislatures and other governmental bodies, and lecturing to any and all groups which wished to consider their doctrines.

Many of the Fabians contributed to the construction of their philosophy and program, but the political, social, and economic beliefs of the society were shaped and phrased primarily by Sidney Webb and, to a lesser degree, by G. B. Shaw. These tenets as expressed in their books and articles—prominent among which were the *Fabian Essays*—show clearly the careful thought, the intelligence, the scholarship, and the deep conviction of their Fabian formulators.

Like the Marxists, the Fabians erect their philosophy on a foundation of historical analysis. This analysis is empirically sound and was, for England at least, prophetically accurate. The essential fact for the Fabians was that the system of economic individualism in England was of such impermanence that almost from its inception it had required regulation and limitation which had intensified as the years went by. Socialism, therefore, was the logical extension of the pattern of controls over economic individualism already prevailing. Such a conclusion, of course, recognizes that change is inherently constant in human relationships and that the trends of change should be carefully guided to socially desirable ends. Stemming from this observation of the dynamic nature of society, the Fabians were critical of the utopians who sought to outline the precepts of an ideal society which would represent a perfectly balanced equilibrium. Instead, said the Fabians, the ideal to be sought is the gradual evolution of society's institutions, consistent with the past traditions and without abrupt change, in the interest of all members of the society. This concept of uninterrupted continuity, peacefully and gradually attained within a constitutional framework, was coupled with an insistence that organic changes can be made only if they are acceptable to the majority of the people. The substitution of socialist economic cooperation for "the anarchy of the competitive struggle" would become a change acceptable to the majority of the people as quickly as education and publicity made clear its desirability.

As had so many others before them, the Fabians recounted at length the ills and vices of the capitalistic system. The sweatshop labor of women and children, the unsanitary conditions of employment, the unconscionable length of the working day, and the use of physical violence to keep the laborer active at his job were among the evils depicted. And to those who objected to socialist schemes as being repugnant to individual independence the Fabians were ready with a startlingly long list of activities from midwifery to interment in which the state already engaged and which were generally accepted without an accompanying feeling that they were stifling independence.

In analyzing the industrial forces tending to socialism William Clarke called attention to the inconsistencies between the results of the factory system and the ideal of freedom which laissez-faire was supposed to exemplify. He noted, for example, that "individualism" was impossible and absurd for the economically pinched worker, and only remedial legislation could prevent his utter demoralization in the impersonal atmosphere of the large industrial enterprise. He noted also that it was futile to talk of the ramifications of a free competitive economy when the reality of the economic arrangement included trusts and monopolies. Going further, Sidney Olivier explained that socialism is the true child of individualism, that it is individualism "rationalized, organized, clothed and in its right mind." In other words, only when man is not distressed and exploited economically can he aspire to the dignity which individualism implies.

The economic theory of the Fabians again departs from the Marxian position. For Marx, the value of any commodity was measured by the amount of labor which went into its production. For the Fabians, the exchange value of a commodity was not so much its labor worth but its utility, and the demand for more useful products could inflate their prices. This concept naturally invalidated the surplus value theme of exploitation which Marx devised. But the Fabians still saw the exploitation from a different vantage point. Since the value of goods produced was created to a large extent by others (demand) rather than by the efforts of the producers themselves (capitalists), private property owners should not be permitted to profit exclusively from such increased value. Yet profits, rents, and interest were precisely this kind of economic gain without the exertion of individual efforts, a gain which should not be privately enjoyed but spread among the workers and even the community as a whole. Under the influence of Henry George, the Fabians were particularly concerned about rents on land whose value was created by the whole community. Such rents, they contended, being socially created should be socially shared rather than accruing to the individual land owner. In fact, socialism simply constituted the process of discontinuing such exactions as were gained without working for them and adding this amount to income derived from labor.

In striving for their objectives the Fabians constantly reiterated the idea that political democracy and socialism were the opposite sides of the same coin—that with the attainment of the former the latter would come automatically. They opposed any kind of independent action by trade unions which would contribute to industrial strife and emphasize the notion of class warfare. Cooperation rather than conflict between classes was the soil from which socialism would grow.

The Fabians did not try to specify in precise detail the structure of the socialist society. They were fond of saying that socialists strive for "ownership of the means of production by the community, and the means of consumption by individuals," but they were reluctant to explain what this would mean except in broad outline. For instance, they foresaw the ownership of the railroads and certain large industries vested in the nation, but land ownership might be vested in smaller social groups. This lack of detail the Fabians felt to be consistent with their ideas of change and continuity, and their criticism of the utopians, and they believed it sufficient to sketch the broad scope of the socialist pattern.

Concerning incentives under socialism Annie Besant attempted to make very clear that the monetary incentive of capitalism was not the only one of importance, and that its modification would not lead to ultimate stagnation of the economy. The immediate— though negative—incentive under socialism would be fear of starvation from unemployment. The shirker, she contended, could just as well be discharged from communal employment as he could from private industry. Further, since the conditions of employment would be made easier, there would be less compulsion for the laborer to reject work. The pressure from fellow workers would also tend to hold the slacker in line. Once the workers felt secure in their subsistence requirements, the desire for wealth and all its implications would be less demanding, and other positive motivations would appear. The desire to excel, to enjoy creativity, to improve, to gain social approval would motivate workers to exert their best energies. And even the instinct of benevolence and the satisfaction of carrying one's share of the load would be brought into play.

SUMMARY

The Fabian Society, beginning in the late nineteenth century, clearly pointed the way which English socialism would follow into the twentieth century. It built its philosophy of socialism on the foundation which had been laid by its predecessor social critics, utopian theorists, and innovating experimenters, and it utilized the actual record of economic regulation, cooperative and trade union growth, and social legislation to rationalize the logic of socialism as the next step resulting from the forces constantly at work in British society. The Fabians rejected the concept of violent revolution to achieve socialist goals and placed their faith in gradualism, continuity, legality, and the democratic process. They did not foresee the eventual obliterations of the political state but its transformation into a prime agency of amelioration for society's masses. They agreed with the Marxists on the exploitative nature of the capitalist economy and the necessity for replacing private ownership with at least a sizeable measure of public ownership, but the crux of this exploitation they found in the notion of economic rent rather than that of surplus value. They viewed the socialist economy not as the defeat of individualism but as providing the minimum economic security essential for the political, social, and psychological manifestations of individualism to flourish. Conformably with their theories of the dynamism of any society, and noting the weakness of the utopian attempt to prescribe the immutable institutions of the ideal community, the Fabians contented themselves with a description of the basic elements and trends of the coming socialist society. And they sought to show that one of the major features of capitalist philosophy—the profit motive, the monetary incentive—could be significantly modified without converting individual workers, technicians, and managers into listless, lazy units in the industrial complex.

The Fabian Society, which consisted for a long while of only a few hundred members and never exceeded a few thousand, set for itself—and succeeded in accomplishing—a rather large task. Through its research and publications, its lectures, and its ventures in practical politics it sought to convert the governing classes to socialism. By its presentation of fact it sought to persuade politicians, executives, civil servants, managerial technicians, and professional men of the virtue of its analysis. And the greatest tribute which can be paid to the soundness of the Fabian approach is the measure of its success. To the extent that the British economy is socialized today, much of the credit must be given to the Society. Labor party pressure in England, whether the party has been in or out of control in Parliament, has affected the degree of nationalization of industry, and the Fabian Society has been influential in Labor party councils. Some appreciation of the impact can be gained from the knowledge that, in 1945, two-thirds of the Labor party's nearly four hundred members in Parliament were simultaneously members of the Fabian Society.

STUDY QUESTIONS AND PROJECT SUGGESTIONS

1. Can the success of Fabian socialism in Great Britain be attributed primarily to that country's democratic traditions?

2. What were the special tactics of the Fabians?

3. Why did the Fabians believe that socialism was the next "logical" step in Britain's economic structure?

4. How did Fabian spokesmen defend the idea that socialism rather than weakening individualism would strengthen it?

5. What was the Fabian position on the relation between "demand" and "profits"?

6. Assess Annie Besant's contention that monetary incentives can be replaced by others equally effective.

7. Summarize the chief features of Fabian socialism.

CHAPTER 6

SYNDICALISM AND GUILD SOCIALISM

Contemporaneously with the development of Fabian socialism in England there came into being in France that branch of the socialist movement known as syndicalism. Essentially, syndicalism (from *syndicat, i.e.* trade union) was a special junction of socialist philosophy and trade union activism liberally seasoned with anarchist doctrine. The roots of these philosophies and activities lay many decades back in French history, and it required the press of historical events and the guidance of outstanding leaders to bring them into fruition and union in the last fifteen years of the nineteenth century.

Despite the fine phrases expressing the spirit of the French Revolution, the establishment of the republic did not afford the French workers the liberty they might have expected. In fact, there was imposed a practical ban on laboring associations which was not lifted until 1884. Nevertheless, the spirit and even the limited practice of trade unionism remained very much alive, and this spirit was nurtured by the various socialist philosophies pronounced over the years. So when the ban on unions was finally removed, the stage was set for the development of a policy and the adoption of a program centering on trade unions as a specific tool of the working classes to improve their lot.

At the same time, French laborers had been exposed to a number of political and economic doctrines which would have a bearing on the course they would follow. The writings of the great utopians had a lasting effect. The cooperative movement had, from time to time, reached new heights of vitality, and hundreds of producers' cooperatives had made their appearance in Paris and the provinces. The anarchism of Proudhon had been complemented by the revolutionary fervor and activity of Louis-Auguste Blanqui who consistently insisted that a militant minority could seize political power. Blanqui's views that private wealth came primarily from immoral sources and that no individual had the right to control exclusively the productive resources of the society were also calculated to enflame passions for the class conflict which he sought.

By 1880, there were several variations of the socialist theme bidding for trade union acceptance and two major personalities competing for philosophical and practical leadership in the socialist movement and the influence it could wield on the *syndicats*. One was Paul Brousse who was dedicated to the proposition that collectivism should be achieved gradually and peacefully through parliamentary process. Brousse and his followers were akin to the independent socialists who, under the leadership of Jean Jaurès, undertook the fostering of legislative measures for the nationalization of industry. Brousse's competitor was Jules Guesde whose outlook was much more revolutionary and Marxian. Guesde denied that the ultimate goal of socialism could be achieved piecemeal or that parliamentary accomplishments represented significant gains. These half-way measures he condemned as being worse than nothing at all because they created an illusion for the masses that permanent progress was being made. Rather, said Guesde, the power of the state must be gained in revolutionary fashion to effect the desired transformation. Some of his followers, it should be noted, were anarchist oriented and desired not merely to seize the political power of the state but to destroy it as a weapon of the capitalist exploiters.

Against this background of dissension, competition, and fragmentation in the labor and socialist ranks there arose in 1892 the *Federation des Bourses du Travail de France*. Individual *Bourses* (Labor Exchanges) had existed since 1887 in Paris, and were designed to serve as headquarters for local unions, bureaus of contact and employment, informational centers, and libraries. The importance of the Federation was its contribution to French syndicalism in the person of its secretary from 1894 to 1901, Fernand Pelloutier, and its advocacy of the general strike as the most important tactic of the working class in achieving its objectives. Eventually the Federation merged with the *Confédération Générale du Travail* thereby losing its organizational autonomy, but the syndicalist concepts espoused by its leaders and supplemented by the intellectual contributions of such writers as Georges Sorel persisted.

Syndicalism accepted basically the Marxian analysis of history with its emphasis upon the economic basis of society's organization. Similarly, the theory of surplus value and the importance of the class struggle are significant elements in syndicalist thought. But on top of this, syndicalism adds certain positive tenets both philosophically and tactically. One such tenet is the virtue of labor. Labor is not merely an act of production for the purpose of gaining wages and earning a living; it is an act of creativity, noble in itself, spiritually satisfying through the sense of accomplishment it induces, and contributory to the development of the total personality. However, under the capitalist wage system with its subsistence levels of remuneration this creative tendency is depressed and thwarted. Being deprived of anything but a menial role in the total productive process the worker becomes not the creative artisan he should be but a drudge who labors in an uninspired and unfulfilling fashion. It is against this situation that labor as a class must struggle.

In terms of tactics the syndicalists reject completely the

precept of progress through parliamentary political process. Instead, revolutionary action is accepted as the only practical road to success. The machinery to be employed in this revolutionary activity is the industrial union and the chief weapon is to be economic pressure which the unions can exert. Syndicalists oppose the development of craft unions as fractionalizing rather than unifying the labor force and the sense of class consciousness which they deem necessary, and because they feel such craft unions to be less effective vehicles for applying the economic pressures envisioned.

As regards the pressures available to the workers through their industrial unions, the syndicalists referred to boycotts, sabotage, and the general strike. Such action was to be taken directly by the workers—under the leadership of a militant minority—but was not necessarily to be always violent. Sabotage could mean actual damage to or destruction of machinery and plant, or it could mean slowdowns, inferior work, or ridiculously literal interpretations of rules and procedures in carrying out job responsibilities. In any event, the end result would be a disarrangement of the orderly flow of goods produced.

The ultimate weapon would be the general strike. It would unleash the full power of all industrial unions in bringing the economic machinery of the society to a halt, and this industrial paralysis would so undermine political and economic authority that the workers could proceed to institute their new regime. Sorel saw the importance of the general strike as "social myth" even if the strike never occurred. As a myth the concept had an organizing and educative force in contributing to the cohesion of the workers, the buoying of their spirits, and the inculcation of the belief that success would crown their efforts. With this spirit, the strike might not be necessary to accomplish the purposes of the organized proletariat.

Consistent with its anarchist tendencies and its Marxian heritage, syndicalist efforts were to be directed not only against the exploiting employers but against the political state as well. Viewing the state not merely as a weapon of exploitation in the hands of the entrepreneurs but as the essence of coercion and restraint on individual freedom, the syndicalists sought its total elimination. They could not agree with their parliamentary socialist brethren that the state should be "captured" and used for socialist purposes; nothing less than its complete obliteration was acceptable. Such political direction as was necessary would then be supplied in small, self-governing communities in which labor councils based on functional representation would be predominant. With the establishment of the new society, workers would own their land and industries in common, they would labor equally with no castes of privilege, and they would share in common the fruits of production.

The extent to which syndicalism attained its vogue in France is probably accounted for by the environment in which it grew. The French tradition of violent insurrection, the French temperament, the need for and respect of intellectual justification of the necessary, the wide acceptance of anarchist theory, and the disappointment of the French workers in socialist leaders who, in practical politics, became enemies of labor all help to explain the conversion of the French to syndicalist doctrine. The more orthodox socialists, of course, challenged syndicalist contentions right down the line. The dangers inherent in ecomonic warfare were clearly delineated, and the virtues of parliamentary gradualism emphatically restated. The vitiating effect of sabotage on the morale of the workers was detailed, and the potential ineffectiveness of the general strike outlined. The incipient conflict between syndicalism's "anti-patriotic" stand and the natural inclination of the citizen was highlighted. Nevertheless, syndicalism retained its strength and exercised a significant influence on the entire socialist movement especially in examining the alternative courses of action open to the working classes in seeking a higher economic and cultural level.

Guild Socialism

The advent of guild socialism was predicated on the existence of a number of disturbing social and economic facts and the propagation of a variety of tracts questioning the propriety of the orthodox socialist approach to the solution of the problems of the people at large. The socialist movement as a whole lent support to the evolution of this special variety in its attack on the wage and profit system, but guild socialists were unable to accept other tenets of their brothers.

The French syndicalists, of course, exercised a strong influence with their anti-state bias and the rejection of normal modes of political action. This position gained strength philosophically from the expostulations of the Reverend J. N. Figgis who attacked the sovereignty of the state as a myth. Figgis' contention was that other organizations existing within the state—including trade unions—had a being and personality separate from the state which were inviolable by state authority.

Beyond this, two categories of publicists helped to push guild socialism to its particular conclusions. The first included such writers as John Ruskin, Thomas Carlyle, and William Morris who harped on the monotony and ugliness of the whole process of factory production and yearned for a return to the years of the guild system in which individual craftsmen taking pride in and deriving satisfaction from their work produced articles not merely of utility but of beauty. This indictment of the factory system was not only on aesthetic grounds but on the grounds that it deprived the worker of the incentive and psychological reward which were legitimately his right.

The second was a group of anti-collectivists led by Gilbert and Cecil Chesterton and Hilaire Belloc who charged capitalism with being materialistic, neglecting quality, and destroying the creative spirit of the workers. At the same time, they indicted socialism on several counts: 1] that it was in the process of creating a "servile state"; 2] that its sponsorship of legislation which made the lot of the workers more endurable supported capitalism and deterred the march of the masses toward their proper goal; and 3] that it limited trade union action through such things as restraints on the right to strike in state-owned industries. In place of either capitalism or socialism these writers argued for a "distributive state" in which the distribution of property among the population would be more equitable. Their ideal was a community composed largely of peasant proprietors whose instinct of ownership would be satisfied by such an arrangement.[1]

So it was that despite the initial successes of the Independent Labour Party based on Fabian principles, guild socialism came to the fore in England. Originated as a movement in 1906 by Arthur J. Penty, an architect, guild socialism soon attracted such prominent leaders as A. R. Orage, S. G. Hobson, a journalist, and G. D. H. Cole, an Oxford fellow who became the ultimate intellectual chief of guild socialism.

An essential premise of the guild socialists was that work had become, at best, a disagreeable necessity which provided neither pleasure nor satisfaction for the worker. The reasons this was so were that work was directed by profiteers and that the specialization of labor had made working monotonous and boring. In short, labor was dehumanized and despiritualized. Thus, the creation of the National Guilds League in 1915 was accompanied by a policy statement setting as goals the abolition of the wage system and the establishment of self-government in industry through a system of national guilds working cooperatively with other democratic functional organizations.

Actually, the ideal of the guild socialists was the re-creation of the qualitative level of achievement which characterized the guild system in the medieval period. In that age the craft guilds had emphasized and taken pride in the high quality of work-

[1] See H. W. Laidler, *A History of Socialist Thought* (New York: T. Y. Crowell Co., 1927), pp. 397-99.

manship of their members, and, at the same time, had sought just price and wages and subjected novices to adequate periods of apprenticeship. Further, the guilds played an important role in the civic and social life of the community.

Unlike the earlier craft guilds, however, the guilds envisioned by the twentieth century guild socialists were to encompass all the workers—manual, technical, or managerial—in a single industry and weld them into a unit of economic and political action. Such guilds were to be national in scope, but local factory management would be the responsibility of local branches of a guild which would also serve as the units from which representatives would be chosen to regional and national bodies. Guilds would, of course, exist not merely for manufacturing processes, but for the distributive, agricultural, and professional aspects of society as well. However, some aspects of societal activity such as journalism and the ministry would not be encompassed in guilds.

It should be emphasized that the reorientation of society along guild lines was not simply an attack on the prevailing economic organization of society but on its political organization as well. The political state was an unnecessary restraint on human freedom, and the guild socialists could not accept the viewpoint of their orthodox fellows that this political apparatus could be transformed into an institution of melioration in the interests of the working classes. Such government as was necessary should be decentralized as much as practicable, and representatives in regional and national guilds should be chosen from local bodies on a functional or occupational basis rather than a geographic basis. Local "communes" composed of guild representatives and representatives from cooperative societies, which were to reflect the wishes of the people as consumers, would guide the economic and social development of the society. While this arrangement would, of course, retain some vestiges of "government," the idea of functional representation and having the "government" closer to the people were more appealing to the guild socialists.

As enunciated by Cole, the guild socialists have little faith in the potentiality of parliamentary procedure to achieve the changes they desire. In the first place there is some question that the working class could be counted on to vote as a bloc in its own behalf. Additionally, to achieve desired change in this manner would take too long and might produce a counter movement in effective opposition. It is also questionable, say the guild socialists, that the fundamental modifications being sought are best brought about by legislative fiat.

Instead of parliamentary action the guild socialists saw an evolutionary process of transition in which the trade unions would play the major role. This was to require a reorganization of both principle and practice in trade unionism. First there was to be the substitution of the industrial for the craft union. Second, the unions were going to have to expand until they possessed a virtual monopoly of the labor market. Then would follow a period of "encroaching control" during which the unions would, step by step, take the organization and management of the industry away from the employers. This would include initially hiring, firing, and disciplining of employees, later, the distribution of wages, still later, the making of policy decisions, and finally the purchase of the industry for its replacement cost. At the same time, some guild socialists believed that certain industries might be nationalized as part of the program of the general transfer of property to the people as a whole. Still others were more closely attuned to the syndicalists in calling for "direct action" methods, including boycotts, strikes, and picketing, as a means of bringing pressure to bear on employers and entrepreneurs.

The guild socialist movement never attracted a large following. The membership of the National Guilds League hovered around 500 members for several years. In the period immediately following World War I, several building guilds were formed in England and performed admirably for several years. They did not, however, survive the industrial depression which followed.

Practically, of course, guild socialism suffered from a number of theoretical and practical shortcomings. For one thing, the concept of superimposing the medieval guild system on the modern industrial structure was a questionable ideal. Furthermore, the guild socialists were, perhaps, carried away with idealizing the older guilds, seeming to overlook the frequently arbitrary and capricious decisions of such guilds and their tendencies to monopoly and its evils. It was also problematical that the political structure of the state could be replaced by a system of communes with any guarantee that the ends sought in the substitution would be attained. In addition, the idiosyncracies of human nature might make unworkable the relationships between a "democratically chosen" manager and his subordinates.

Nevertheless, despite its weaknesses and its relatively small number of adherents, guild socialism made a significant impact on socialist theory generally. The movement emphasized the potential for industrial action, it minimized to a degree the harshness of syndicalism and introduced instead a modicium of gradualism, it questioned the dangers in bureaucratic collectivism and centralized authority, it highlighted the principle of functional representation, and it spoke for an increased role for the actual producers in the management of the productive process. Not only this, but a number of its special goals—the role of the shop steward, labor-management bargaining, and the closed shop—became an accepted part of modern industrial relations.

STUDY QUESTIONS AND PROJECT SUGGESTIONS

1. To what extent was French syndicalism a product of the environment in which it grew?

2. Analyze the contention in syndicalism and guild socialism that in the capitalist factory system aesthetic creativity and psychological satisfaction are denied the average worker.

3. Write a brief essay on Georges Sorel's elaboration of the general strike as social myth.

4. Outline the major precepts of the syndicalist program of "direct action" by workers in attaining their goals, and compare these with the beliefs of the guild socialists.

5. Compare and contrast the characteristics of the medieval guild system with the economic and political characteristics of society as visualized by the guild socialists.

6. Discuss briefly the theoretical and practical contributions of guild socialism to the general socialist movement.

CHAPTER 7

COMMUNISM (MARXISM)

Though not, strictly speaking, a kind of "socialism" as originally delineated, some attention should be given to Marxism because of the impact which it had on socialist development. In some respects, of course, communism is closely related to socialism. Like socialism it attacks the basic tenets of capitalism; both seek a degree of transference of private property to public ownership; both reject the inequities of income distribution in a free enterprise society; both insist on a renovation of society along collectivist lines. But, as previously noted, there are important differences in essential principles, in the process of change envisioned, and in the nature of the revised society. Possibly the major impetus which the Marxist philosophy gave to socialism was the fervor which was implanted in the hearts of collectivist leaders generally.

The communist ideology is essentially the concoction of Karl Marx and Friedrich Engels whose *Communist Manifesto* swept Europe in 1848. Marx' later work, *Das Kapital*, published in three volumes between 1867 and 1895, was a much more monumental task, though it may not have had the penetrating effect of the earlier pamphlet. At any rate, in his various publications Marx makes a ringing—if at times inaccurate—indictment of capitalist economics.

Marx bases his approach to the proper economic organization of society on a sweeping analysis of history in which economic motives are predominant. To Marx history unfolds as the progression of forces which generate internally, as they develop, competing forces which ultimately cause modification of the original force. This concept—known as the dialectic—postulates that every historical tedency (a thesis) in the course of its evolution must inevitably produce a tendency of inner contradiction (an antithesis) which will just as inevitably bring about the destruction or extreme modification of the initial tendency thus producing a novel tendency (a synthesis). What is particularly important—from the Marxist point or view—is the inescapability of this series of events. It is the "law" of history and lends the force of historical imperative to the analysis which Marx proceeds to make within this framework. What he describes becomes then not only desirable but inevitable.

The basic human endeavor, contends Marx, has always been to sustain human existence. In other words, man's primary activity has been to wrest a living from his physical environment—to feed, clothe, and house himself and his family. As men combine in groups and form societies, the methods adopted to produce and distribute goods and services will induce the creation of economic and social patterns and organizations compatible with the methods chosen. That is, economic and social systems exhibiting rather consistent characteristics will result from the nature of the mode of producing and distributing those commodities and services—on a constantly recurring basis—which the community requires to sustain itself. Social classes will then develop in terms of the positions held by the members of such classes in the economic system, and political machinery which reflects the viewpoints and attitudes of the *dominant* economic class will come into being.

In short, Marx insists that the total structure of any society—its political, legal, social, and cultural characteristics—will be determined by the *economic* base and pattern of that society. All other aspects of societal living will be directly or indirectly influenced and shaped by economic motives and activity. Marx admits that there are other forces in history such as ideals, prominent personalities and leaders, and spiritual convictions which may affect the development of society's institutions; but he argues that even these have been initially produced and directed by more fundamental economic and material factors.

The different classes which the society produces, Marx continues, are naturally antagonistic, each seeking to obtain for itself greater economic benefits, normally at the expense of the other classes. Such strife and competition between classes begins in and, originally, may be confined to the economic arena, but eventually it verges over into the political arena as well. In this contest, the dominant economic class naturally uses all the weapons at its command—economic, political, and, perhaps, military— to maintain the status quo and perpetuate its position of privilege. Since this dominant but "outmoded" economic class fails to recognize the changed circumstances requiring its elimination and refuses to surrender peaceably and gracefully to the demands of the "emerging" new class, the latter has no alternative but to seize power by force and violence so as to reshape the economic and political features of society as it deems best.

In the era of capitalist economics Marx sees the issues as being particularly clear. There are two prevalent classes—the capitalist exploiting group and the masses of the people (the proletariat) who are exploited. The degree of this exploitation is explained in terms of the theory of "surplus value." The surplus value concept postulates that the true value of any commodity produced should be measured by the amount of labor which has gone into its production. However, says Marx, the market value of a commodity generally exceeds its "labor value" because of the failure of the capitalists to pay labor its fair wage for its role in production. Instead, labor receives only a subsistence level wage far lower than what it should get for its share in the productive process. In other words, the amount paid for labor as a resource in production is inadequate, and the value created by labor exceeds the cost of the labor power which is consumed. This excess or surplus value is appropriated by the capitalist in the form of profits, interest, or rents.

It is, of course, against this state of affairs that the exploited class is urged to fight. This analysis is also illustrative of the dialectical approach which Marx used. The nature of capitalism is such, say the Marxists, that the capitalist class tends to enrich itself more and more at the expense of the proletariat, widening the gulf between wealth and poverty, minimizing the number of wealthy and increasing the number of poor, solidifying this relationship, and, in the process, making the proletariat more conscious of itself as a class, creating—if inadvertently—a growing desire on the part of the proletariat to improve its lot, and finally—by its very intransigence—supplying the spark which will push the proletariat to the revolutionary action which will cause the transformation of capitalism (as a thesis) into a new economic and political arrangement.

As though the "inherent contradiction" of the developing proletariat were not enough, Marx sees corollary developments which will inevitably contribute to capitalism's downfall. As the wealth of the entrepreneurs increases, the consuming power of the working classes decreases relatively, thus making it less likely that total production can be absorbed effectively by the society. Still, production tends to increase at the insistence of the capitalists who seek constantly greater profits. In the end, then, despite luxury production, credit sales, intricate financial arrangements, and the development of new markets over-production and depression with all its miseries must result.

In addition, such a theoretically effective characteristic of capitalism as competition degenerates into monopoly, thereby destroying the advantages which competition offers to the consumer and the impetus to improved productive practices. Simultaneously, the various capitalist powers soon find themselves engaged in strenuous competition for external markets which will periodically erupt into overt warfare. Such crises as these, plus the natural workings of the dialectic process, must inevitably bring about capitalism's downfall.

Strangely enough, for the Marxists, the internal contradictions, the modification of natural characteristics, and the periodic crises which trumpet the "inevitable" fall of the capitalist system of its own weight are still insufficient. The proletariat must still accept the responsibility for initiating a successful revolution to dislodge the well-entrenched capitalists and wrest from them control of the means of production and distribution.

Once the revolution has achieved the destruction of the capitalists, the victorious proletariat will proceed with the establishment of a socialist state, the cornerstone of which will be the common (public) ownership of the means of production and distribution. The entire economic activity of the society will be organized on a highly planned basis in which centralized authority will be predominant. Work will be available for all—and will be expected of all. As a matter of fact, one of the shibboleths of the communist philosophy is: "From each according to his ability; to each according to his needs." In this new culture all economic and social classes will be abolished; all will be "workers"; there will be no exploiters and no exploited. Economic security is thus to be assured, and, at the same time, the communists claim that every possible degree of individual freedom —consistent with national and economic security—will be afforded.

The transition from the capitalist to the socialist economy and the ultimate millennium will involve some political as well as military maneuvering. The presumed military victory must be followed, say the communists, by the establishment of a "temporary" dictatorship of the proletariat to prevent any counter-revolution and to insure the inauguration of the new program. Eventually, however, the communists foresee the "withering away" of the political state which they continue to view as a weapon of potential exploitation. Instead, all that will remain is a structure of administrative agencies required to run the publicly owned economy. (To what extent this administrative structure with, presumably, the power of decision-making would differ from "government" or a "political apparatus" seems questionable.)

Nicolai Lenin

These essential features of the basic communist ideology received certain refinement and redirection from a number of sources over the years, a chief contributor being Vladimir Ilyich Ulyanov—or Nicolai Lenin. Lenin's contribution was much more as an organizer and activist, but as a theorist he made some major modifications in the communist ideology which served not only as tools in the successful Russian revolution but became parts of the essential beliefs of dedicated communists. Lenin always viewed theory as a set of guidelines rather than a body of static doctrine—a tentative blueprint, not an intellectual strait-jacket confining rather than liberating action. To him, tactics coming from theory must always remain flexible, so that the best use could be made of any existing circumstances.

One central theoretical problem which concerned Lenin was the exact nature of the revolutionary ferment which was to lead to the new regime. Unlike his Menshevik opponents, Lenin did not see the "revolution" as a more or less spontaneous organization of the working classes for political action on the legal level. He could not accept an essentially decentralized organization of trade unions as providing the necessary impetus to class conflict and triumph. Actually, Lenin saw the achievement of trade unionism as the outer limit of the intellectual capacity and aspiration of the working class; the implications of a socialist revolution were beyond them. Since the trade unions then were incapable of developing for themselves an adequate revolutionary ideology, such ideology would have to be developed for them by middle class intellectuals. Workers would have to be indoctrinated, in other words, by certain leaders (traitors?) from the middle class, part of which at least was doomed to extinction by the successful revolution. Thus the working class which supposedly had its mentality formed and its goals set by its economic and social position in society was, in fact, to be directed and led to its emancipation by a middle class intelligentsia.

Further, Lenin visualized the vanguard of the revolutionary movement as an inner group of professional revolutionaries, rigidly disciplined and tightly organized, acting as a conspiratorial underground spearhead. This vanguard—the communist party and, more particularly, its leadership element—was to be an intellectual elite in defining doctrine and providing policy guidance, and it was to be a moral elite in that its selection and training would give it a complete devotion to the purposes of the revolution. The potentialities for an increasing centralization of authority in this concept is, of course, obvious, and its compatibility with the idea of a dictatorship of the proletariat as part of the revolutionary activity is similarly observable.

One further point of interest should be noted. The Marxian thesis is that capitalism produces the urban proletariat which will in time prove to be the undoing of capitalism. While this then might well hold in the highly industrialized countries of western Europe, the size of this body in Russia made it apparent to Lenin that an appeal would also have to be made to the Russian peasants and agricultural workers if a successful revolution was to be launched. What is particularly intriguing about this development is that in 1963-64 the "ideological" debate between the leaders of the Soviet Union and Red China finds the former accusing the latter of "revisionism" for having emphasized peasant support in the Chinese upheaval, and the latter accusing the former of failing to recognize the "new road" to socialism. While it can be safely asumed that this most recent conflict involved less ideology than it did competing national interests and the respective aspirations of Nikita Khrushchev and Mao Tse-tung to be recognized as *the* leader of the world communist movement, it is a bit odd to see much of the argumentation phrased in an idiom which ignores the role of the Russian peasantry in the communist revolution leading to the establishment of the current Soviet regime.

One other "ideological" contribution might be mentioned here, stemming from the long-time Soviet dictator, Joseph Stalin. While Stalin accepted essentially the Marxist-Leninist version of the communist ideology, the nature of the Soviet Union of which Stalin found himself in control and the nature of the world situation during his period of leadership prompted him to emphasize two points of "philosophical" modification. The first was a concentration on "socialism in one country." Thus the communist revolution became, at least temporarily, not so much a worldwide movement as a struggle to insure the stabilization of the socialist system in the Soviet Union itself. The second modification was the enunciation of the doctrine of "capitalist encirclement." This doctrine had the dual utility of supporting the concept of socialism in one country and, more important, justifying the maintenance of the police state and the dictatorial policies which Stalin sought to perpetuate in his own interest. So long as the Soviet Union was surrounded by hostile capitalist states, every effort must be made to safeguard socialist institutions and to prevent internal subversion.

Criticisms of Communist Theory

A general discussion of the pros and cons of socialism will follow later, but at this point a special consideration of some of the inconsistencies of communist theory and practice might be in order. The impact which communist theory and action has had around the world seems to be based in part on the failure to recognize certain basic shortcomings of this ideology, and a recognition of its faults is surely imperative.

To begin with, if the validity of the dialectic process is accepted, why is such elaborate revolutionary planning necessary? If capitalism's internal inconsistencies and crises foredoom it to collapse, presumably there is no need for a proletarian uprising. If, on the other hand, the dialectic is merely a "working hypothesis," as Engels maintained, which still required conscious planning and action to instigate, then the communists can hardly claim the force of historical imperative in their position. Nor can it be explained that revolutionary planning and action are merely hastening the inevitable, for Marx insisted that capitalism would have to run its full course before the era of communism could be ushered in. Thus it can be seen that the communist theme begins on a contradictory note—a claim of inevitable development and simultaneously an emphasis on the absolute need for revolutionary action. Furthermore, assuming any validity to the dialectic analysis, why would communism be necessarily the ultimate end of the evolutionary process?

A second question might be legitimately raised about the tactic of revolution itself as the most suitable road to the attainment of the goals which the communists supposedly seek. Are the tactics of revolution compatible with the inculcation of the ideals essential for the practical working of the communistic society? Can large scale violence contribute to the release and development of those human qualities needed in the communist state, or would communism require the restraint of exactly those emotions which violence releases? Revolutionary savagery is surely not consistent with the serene cooperation envisaged in the socialist society. In short, by insisting on a path of violence the communists seem to be creating additional obstacles to the achievement of the system advocated.

Is an analysis of history—pointing to a foreordained conclusion—based exclusively on economic factors really viable? Is "economic man" the true picture of the typical human being? Are there not other aspects of the human spirit and man's environment which modify and moderate Marx' economic analysis? And if this is so does this not undercut not only the Marxist assumptions but the predicted historical evolution? In fact, does not the history of capitalist evolution in the century since Marx invalidate many of his conclusions?

As regards the temporary nature of the proletarian dictatorship and the eventual withering away of the political state, the empirical evidence of the Soviet Union itself serves as an adequate commentary. After half a century of existence there is little to suggest that the dictatorship of the communist party and its leadership is on the verge of being replaced by anything approaching a democratic political process. Though the techniques may be less brutal, the reins of authority are still as tightly held. But beyond this, it would be an absurd tax on one's imagination to picture the voluntary relinquishing of power by the likes of those who have served as leaders since the Soviet revolution and a similar voluntary consenting to the dissolution of the political apparatus through which power has been maintained. Even if one were capable of such visualization, the necessary retention of administrative machinery for the direction of the society's economy would still parallel the duties and the authority of the political state.

Other questions which might be raised of both communism and socialism include the relationship between economic regimentation and personal freedom; the effect on initiative and ambition in a society which rewards its workers according to "need"; the selection of those who will define and delineate respective needs; the necessity for class conflict rather than cooperation; and the potential attainment of a "classless" society in any event.

The U.S.S.R. Economy Today

The economy of the Soviet Union can be described as "communistic" only in terms of the extent to which economic arrangements are socialized, i.e., the degree to which practically all economic forces are owned, supervised, and directed by the state. There is certainly no absence of political machinery which the communist millennium promises. There is no "classlessness" in the Soviet society, and gradations in economic and social status, position and privilege, opportunity and luxury, which rival anything in capitalism are readily observable—despite the common appellation of "comrade." The principle of "from each according to his ability; to each according to his needs" remains "on the drawing board." Instead, economic incentives not unlike those found in a capitalist society are widely utilized to induce higher and better production among workers. Planning has not resulted in a nice neat balance in the production of goods and services, and the "communist" society has been plagued with many of the difficulties which have at times beset capitalist economies. In short, the "communist panacea" for the economic ills of capitalism has turned out to be neither communist nor a panacea.

The central feature of the Soviet economy is its centralized direction by the communist party leadership to serve the purposes which the leadership defines. While the "state" owns just about every phase of the economic apparatus—industrial, agricultural, and distributive—the use to which the economic machinery will be put is decided by a small inner circle of party leaders. Within this broad framework the essential details of production and distribution are worked out by a central planning agency, Gosplan. Below this, finer points of the productive process may be refined on a more decentralized basis even to the level of individual factory managers who are responsible for meeting production quotas. Soviet economic goals have been generally set forth in a series of five-year plans which emphasize special efforts in various branches of the economy.

A second major feature of the Soviet economy has been its absolute drive for rapid industrialization, particularly in the field of heavy industry. Such industry was to be the foundation of broad economic development as well as the cornerstone of national power in line with the Soviet position as a great nation and its expansionist aspirations. Thus, resources were allocated arbitrarily to this end with the corollary result that consumer goods production continued to drag and the general living standard remained low and static. Only recently has there begun an upswing in living standards for the average Soviet citizen.

The collectivization of the Soviet economy takes many forms and has undergone numerous modifications through the years since the revolution. In industry, the backbone of production has been the state factories, mines, etc., though industrial cooperatives have played a significant role in the consumer goods area, and there are some individual artisans working in specialized fields, particularly the creative arts. In agriculture both state farms and collective farms have been used, and both have had their problems. Compensation varies tremendously for different kinds of labor, and incentives of various sorts, such as bonuses, are used regularly to stimulate greater production or improved labor techniques. Occasionally the communist leadership has found it necessary to relax the degree of control over the economy and permit a bit of the "capitalist spirit" to erupt in order to rejuvenate the economic process.

As is true of American business and industry, the Soviet Union has long recognized the role which the effective manager can play in production, and it has worked hard to train such a managerial cadre. On the whole, the Soviet manager tends to be more engineering oriented and more formally educated than his American counterpart, but each plays a significant role in his respective enterprise, and each is more highly compensated than the average worker. The Soviet manager's discretion is more limited and he is probably less adept at "human relations," but he has become part of a bureaucratic class which may have a lasting impact on the Soviet society.

In general, then, we may view the Soviet economy as highly collectivized, centrally planned, and politically directed. It is an economy in which heavy industrialization has proceeded at a rapid rate and in which consumer goods production has risen. The high level of Soviet education and technology is amply demonstrated by its accomplishments in the space sciences as well as its rate of economic growth. In agriculture, interesting innovations have been tried, but increasing agricultural production remains as a significant problem for a nation with a growing population. But this base of collectivism remains overlaid with a goodly measure of capitalist incentives, income disparities, competition, and striving to excel.

STUDY QUESTIONS AND PROJECT SUGGESTIONS

1. Outline the dialectic process which Marx used to make his interpretation of history.
2. What inferences does Marx draw from his belief in economic influences in life?
3. In addition to the evolution of the proletariat, what other factors does Marx see as contributing to the downfall of capitalism?
4. Describe the nature of the communist society which will, according to Marxism, supposedly replace the capitalistic type.
5. What particular contributions did Lenin make to communist theory and practice?
6. Discuss briefly those elements of communist ideology and tactics which suggest its validity as a doctrine or societal system.
7. Outline the ways in which and the reasons why the economy of the U.S.S.R. has become more "capitalistic" in recent years.

CHAPTER 8

SOCIALISM
IN AMERICA

We have already noted that utopian socialism found many supporters in the United States and that this country was the locale for a number of experiments in communal living based on the utopian theories. We have further recognized that Christian socialism was upheld by many vocal advocates in America. Beyond this, however, socialism of a more orthodox variety and even socialism with a revolutionary tinge flourished for a time in the United States and had quite an effect on political and economic theory and action from the latter part of the nineteenth century. It should be added further that the United States has had for many years a full-fledged communist party, committed to Marxian principles and seemingly reflecting the political lead of the Soviet Union, but the history of this group is beyond the scope of this study.

Orthodox American socialism presumably had its beginnings with the immigration of German socialists following the uprisings of the 1830's and 1840's. Such socialists began to influence the thinking of workingmen, and by 1877 there was organized the Socialist Labor party as a vehicle for action. By 1892 this group nominated a presidential ticket, and by the time of the elections of 1898, Socialist Labor candidates received in excess of 80,000 votes. But the party was destined for difficulties in the form of leadership squabbles. Daniel DeLeon and others began to insist more and more that the party should foster industrial unions rather than craft unions (as the syndicalists and guild socialists had desired) as the most effective trade union organization for the furthering of labor's objectives. Such leaders as Job Harriman and Morris Hillquit, however, believed that the socialists should continue to cooperate with the existing labor organizations. DeLeon ultimately became a leader in the Industrial Workers of the World, an organization created in 1905.

In the interim, another group under the leadership of Eugene V. Debs formed, in 1897, the Social Democracy of America which became, the following year, the Social Democratic party of America. In 1900 a cooperative position was reached between this new grouping and the Harriman-Hillquit forces of the Socialist Labor party. Under the arrangement Debs was nominated for the presidency of the United States and Harriman for the vice-presidency. In the presidential election which followed, the ticket garnered almost 98,000 popular votes. In 1901, following another convention at Indianapolis, the temporarily aligned socialist groups became officially the Socialist party in the United States.

Before examining further the political activities and the philosophy of the American Socialist party, we might take a quick glance at the position of the Industrial Workers of the World. Basically, the I.W.W. was an American expression of syndicalism appealing primarily to the unskilled workers who were denied participation in the more exclusive craft unions of the American Federation of Labor. Lumber workers, longshoremen, and agricultural migrant workers were among its chief adherents, with its principal organizational unit being the Western Federation of Miners. Though its membership never exceeded 100,000, the militancy of the I.W.W. was calculated to appeal emotionally to large numbers of workers concerned with the ambling pace of progress in improving labor's economic position in American society.

The I.W.W. sought a proliferation of industrial unions as the means of bringing pressure to bear on and wringing concessions from recalcitrant employers. On the whole, these American exponents of syndicalism were somewhat less anarchistic and less violent than their French counterparts, but their techniques engendered violence nevertheless. While industrial sabotage was not officially sanctioned, it was practiced by some members. The concept of the general strike was prominent in I.W.W. thinking, and many ordinary strikes were initiated and carried out for short periods. As it evolved, the I.W.W. became more proletarian in character and more critical of socialist theorists and intellectuals; it insisted on programs of industrial action.

The United States entry into World War I in 1917 faced the I.W.W. with a crisis from which it never recovered. The membership was divided between patriotic support of the war effort and socialistic opposition to capitalist warfare. There was similar dissension relating to the question of approval or disapproval of the revolution in Russia. Further, the government took a dim view of strikes or other disturbances which would interfere with our war potential, and such I.W.W. activities were met with military force. When the burden of post-war unemployment was added and an unfriendly legal atmosphere tended to limit the I.W.W.'s actions, the organization lapsed into impotency.

The Socialist party, in the meantime, continued to grow in popular support and continued to nominate a presidential candidate whose popular vote grew from 400,000 in 1904 to just under a million in 1920. Eugene Debs was the perennial candidate, with the exception of 1916 when Allan Benson was the nominee. In the 1924 election the Socialists supported the La-Follette-Wheeler ticket of the Progressive party which received close to five million popular votes. Two years later, Debs, wearied by his efforts and terms in federal prison, died at the age of seventy. Norman Thomas succeeded to the leadership of the Socialist party and was its presidential nominee in 1928 and on five subsequent occasions.

Because of opposition to American participation in World War I, the Socialist party lost much of its comparatively small ideological support in the United States, and many of its members, including Debs, were sent to jail. This dual assault on popularity and organizational leadership signaled the decline of socialist appeal in America which was further confirmed by the growing prosperity of the 1920's. The apparent popular support evidenced by the presidential votes seems properly interpreted as a result of Debs' personal ability and magnetism rather than an endorsement of socialist doctrine. These things, together with the constant internal strife and fractionalization of socialistically inclined groups, doomed American socialism as such, despite its brief revival under Thomas in the depression days of the 1930's.

American socialism, particularly as represented by Debs, was fairly orthodox socialism with its condemnation of a capitalist system which concentrated the tools of production in the hands of a few and left the average worker so much at the mercy of the entrepreneur. It assailed the profit motive, private ownership, the lack of competition in many areas of the economy and called for public ownership of productive facilities and the use of governmental machinery in the transformation of society. At one time Debs spoke of socialism as a political movement of the working class aiming at the overthrow of the capitalist system— "changing a republic in name into a republic in fact." "The earth for all the people! That is the demand." Going on, Debs reiterated the frequently heard demands for the elimination of minority control of the machinery of production and distribution; the collectivization of industry and democratic management; the elimination of rent, interest and profit; the end of class struggles through the amalgamation of competing forces; and the creation of a new social order.

Norman Thomas' succession to the leadership of the Socialist party represented some modification of Debs' militancy. As ideological spokesman for American socialists Thomas could not escape the influence of his early environment or his own temperament, and, as a result, socialist dogma in the United States became temporarily unique. As a minister and the son of a minister, as a practicing social worker, and as something of a pacifist, Thomas was attracted to socialism's attack on social injustice, but he was also nurtured in an environment which might lead him to question the more materialistic and militant aspects of socialist doctrine. As resolutely as he might oppose "imperialistic" conflict, Thomas did reject the Marxian concept of class warfare. While his background could be expected to produce in him a missionary zeal in the pursuit of his goals, it would similarly lead him to examine carefully the means chosen to achieve the ends in terms of his Christian orientation.

Thomas could not accept the tyranny of the Soviet system, nor could he willingly embrace the ideological dogma which limited man's creativity and ingenuity. As a matter of fact, Thomas' concept of social change was imprecise and he was as much a supporter of specific "liberal" objectives—social security, minimum wage and maximum hour legislation, improved rights for labor—as he was of a broad socialist program. He was less an architect of a total socialist platform than he was a contributor to the temper and attitude of his times—a temper and attitude which manifested itself more successfully in related social and political movements than in socialism itself, though, to be sure, Thomas did subscribe to the essential socialist tenet of state ownership of an appreciable segment of major industries.

Of particular significance as a distinguishing feature of Thomas' position was the appeal which he had for the middle class. He was himself a product of that class, spoke the language of the class, and saw in the middle class a strong force which could be invoked to bring about the change in the intellectual and social environment which he sought. While, perhaps, pragmatically accurate in appraising the strength of the middle class in the United States and counting on its support rather than seeking a proletarian revolution, in pitching his appeal at this level Thomas was more effective in making converts for progressivism than for socialism per se. If this be the case, then Norman Thomas can be credited with a sizeable—though inadvertent—contribution to minimizing socialist influence in this country while creating an atmosphere in which social change more in line with American traditions could occur.

Thomas' natural predisposition toward the middle class made him naturally antagonistic to the communist concept of the elimination of that class as a bourgeois grouping. Presumably he could envision the absorption of the middle class into an ultimate classless society, but he could not see the middle class—especially in the United States—as an "enemy" of the socialist movement. As a fact Thomas viewed the lower middle class as being on the verge of proletarianism economically and the upper middle class as being more sympathetically allied with social reform than the maintenance of the capitalist status quo.

As a socialist Thomas concerned himself extensively with the propositions of Karl Marx. He was able to see in Marx' economic analysis of history a significant effort to explain human action and human motivation which found verification in America's depression of the 1930's. But he was forced to question the all-embracing economic theme which Marx postulated (and the conclusions which Marx drew therefrom) and to ask if human nature was basically involved as opposed to the nature of the capitalist society in which human nature had to function. Thomas even saw the value of the Marxian analysis of the class struggle as a description of the major economic forces in the society and as a "concept" which might serve to solidify the working classes in their march toward socialism. He saw further that the harshness of the analysis could act as a shield against becoming mesmerized by pious platitudes coupled with inaction in the area of social and economic reform. At the same time, however, Thomas rejected the class struggle as a reality. He opposed the physical violence and chaos which he felt would result from the revolution advocated by Marx. Similarly, the thorough validity of the surplus value concept of exploitation was recognized as something less than a "scientific" basis for overt upheaval in any society.

In the final analysis, Norman Thomas' broad definition of socialism consisted of a modicum of public ownership of the means of production joined with a considerable amount of pragmatic planning in the economic sphere, the entire mixed economic apparatus operating within a framework of democracy and humanitarianism. In this scheme Thomas saw planning as the key but not as the cure-all. He recognized the virtues inherent in the competition and diversity of the private segment of the economy and was wise enough to question the effects which the restraints of planning might have on such virtues. Was a high degree of planning compatible with personal freedom? With political democracy? Or must it lead to a burdensome regimentation and orthodoxy? In view of the difficulty of discovering "final" answers to these questions, Thomas held that socialism must avoid dogmatism, that it must retain flexibility and adaptability. This is hardly the blind faith and dedicated action of the orthodox socialist reared in economic determinism. Thomas is not the picture of the revolutionary activist—impatient, headstrong, abrupt, and distinctly convinced that socialism is the path and the task of the exploited masses. Thomas' socialism is one of moderation, of compromise and concession, of intelligent analysis of political, economic, and social forces in his own environment.

In a way, this position for all its mildness and broad appeal— probably far wider than was indicated by electoral support— was self-defeating. Even this mood of moderation left socialism as an unsavory idea to most Americans. But Thomas' position— both in terms of ideals and empiric goals—made a contribution to a climate in which other movements of the late nineteenth and early twentieth centuries, subscribing in part to the same program as the socialists, made headway in the United States. A socialist America was not in the cards, despite the efforts of Debs and Thomas. However, the progressive era and programs which socialism helped to generate, and the New Deal era of the 1930's effectuated some of socialism's limited objectives and defined new techniques which permitted government to exercise a restraining hand on the exploitative abuses of capitalism while retaining the basic capitalist structure with its real advantages.

STUDY QUESTIONS AND PROJECT SUGGESTIONS

1. Outline the organizational development of the Socialist party in the United States.

2. What was the role of the International Workers of the World in the evolution of American socialism?

3. From an examination of the speeches and writings of Eugene Debs compile a summary of his basic beliefs as an American socialist.

4. Discuss the propostion that Norman Thomas' background hindered him from becoming a typically orthodox socialist.

5. Analyze the contention that American socialism, in assisting in the attainment of limited labor objectives, undercut the potential for a truly socialist movement in the United States.

CHAPTER 9

PROGRESSIVISM
AND THE NEW DEAL

The socialist movement in the United States was part of and gave inadvertent sustenance to a broader politico-economic upheaval originating in the latter part of the nineteenth century. The evolution of American capitalism had brought with it some real abuses and some imagined injuries which instigated a farmer-labor movement designed to limit such abuses and to create a positive atmosphere for the economic improvement of the two groups concerned. As politicians, journalists, jurists, and others interested themselves in this development, America became immersed in that philosophy and program of action known as progressivism. And it was the spirit of this era which subsequently motivated the political program which came to be known as the New Deal. If we are to evaluate realistically the impact of American socialism we must examine the effects of the progressive era and the New Deal, because, while neither can be identified correctly as being "socialistic," the practical attainments of both reflect in part the spirit and objectives of American socialists.

Defining the "progressive era" presents something of a difficulty because it was as much a spirit as it was a program of practical accomplishments. It was a more or less natural response to an existing social and economic environment, but it developed for itself a philosophy of objective and process which transcended the limits of that environment. It sought tangible goals for specific groups, but it drew support from persons unaffiliated with the groups concerned. It borrowed from alien ideologies and programs, but it was shaped in the American tradition. It was liberal in outlook, but its liberalism was modified by the restraints of tradition. It attempted to harmonize political democracy with economic autocracy in a synthesis which would not do irreparable damage to either. It sought to humanize the industrial order without resort to extreme measures which could undermine the American economic system without guaranteeing the achievement of the humanitarian aims desired. It sought a reorientation of property rights and income distribution as established under capitalism without a destruction of the inherent virtues of that system. In its evolution the progressive movement affected not only economics and politics, but religion, sociology, philosophy, and the arts. Practitioners in all of these disciplines found themselves involved directly or indirectly in the mental and emotional upheaval which the movement represented. The breadth and variety of the movement did not, however, deprive it of focus—a concentration on social and economic reform along ethical lines.

More rigorously and systematically examined, progressivism's essential characteristics can be more clearly delineated. In the first place there was widespread criticism of the laissez-faire system and the social relations stemming from it. The realities of exploitation of human and natural resources, the harshness of the competitive system, the tendency to monopoly, and the waste and inefficiency were brought into the spotlight and weighed against the seeming advantages of the system. To many, this unveiling of realities seemed to call for placing limits on the free play of the economy—for introducing at least some degree of governmental regulation to curb the inadequacies and abuses in the system. Simultaneously the question was raised as to the desirability of measuring a man's worth—his intelligence, ability, respectability, and social standing—in terms of business acumen and the accumulation of wealth. Was it good for a society to emphasize material success as its prime criterion for gauging prominence, or did this emphasis on acquisitiveness depreciate other criteria of greater significance in the long run? For many progressives this unrelenting pursuit of riches in self-interest (often coupled with their attainment through corruption and dishonesty) was unworthy and even dangerous. Instead, they counseled self-sacrifice and a life of service. Material comforts and a better living standard were not condemned, but seeking after them as life's major goal and the concentration of so much wealth in the hands of a few were.

"Exposure" was another characteristic of the progressive movement. The "muckrakers" were dedicated not only to an exposition of the actualities of the capitalist system but to an uncovering of the extent of graft and corruption in state and local governments and the unholy alliances which existed in many cases between corrupt officials and industrial entrepreneurs. Such muckraking seems to have been inspired as a criticism of the societal environment as well as a criticism of specific shortcomings of the capitalist economic system. The progressive era was also a period of iconoclasm. Legends and traditions which had developed and stood for years were subjected to a new scrutiny. Here again, the motive appears to have been a feeling on the part of the iconoclasts that Americans should view themselves and their forebears realistically—stripped of the myths which inevitably seem to generate about the past. Only such a realistic appraisal would point the way to future progress.

In keeping with the general theme of the period, ethics and the spirit of Christianity were elevated to new planes of prominence as bases for evaluating the mores of the society and for charting the course of reform. The social Darwinism of Herbert Spencer and others which taught the law of the jungle in social and economic life began to be overshadowed by concern with one's fellow man. The Christian spirit of love as opposed to the selfishness of the American social milieu gained new strength and new advocates. It was even recognized that such outlook did not betoken weakness or a utopian desire to remake the world, but a simple urge to modify society within practical limits in line with the Christian ethic and for the benefit of larger numbers of people. This humanitarian impulse in progressivism manifested itself in the setting of significant but limited goals—factory inspection and improved safety devices, better schools, special protection for women and children in the economic arena, prison reform, and temperance. Such objectives were not visionary, but they required a social and economic reorientation for Americans in which government might have to play a decisive role.

The cry for renovation in the progressive era was probably an inescapable response to the economic environment which had itself undergone such drastic change in the previous decades. The self-employed artisan and the small shop or business had been replaced by the large corporation in which the individual worker became more and more a unit of production rather than a personality. Not only was the worker depersonalized in thought and relation to his enterprise, but management became less aware of him as an individual. In this context workers' characters as well as their economic well being suffered. Concepts of minimum wage and maximum hours laws—enforced by governmental authority—began to take shape. Unionization as a tool for collective bargaining with employers and a greater voice in their respective endeavors appealed increasingly to rank and file employees. And adverse Supreme Court decisions regarding the constitutionality of economic legislation—based on the Court's idea of what constituted "freedom of contract"—did not stem the march.

Democracy as a way of life and as a political process also came to be reexamined closely in the period. Was the American version of democracy living up to the promise inherent in this humane philosophy of contributing to the dignity of the human being and helping to elevate him to the highest spiritual and temporal plane of which he was capable? Was the concept of majority rule compatible with economic aristocracy? Did a democratic society have a responsibility to alleviate the problems of the masses of the people? And did the political process then existing offer an adequate avenue of approach to the solution of those problems which plagued so many members of the society? The answers which progressivism found for such questions argued strongly for positive action on the part of government; neutrality would simply contribute to the perpetuation of the status quo.

This introspection led many progressive spokesmen to call for a greater amount of "direct" democratic action—an enlargement of the electorate and a more effective voice for that electorate in policy decisions. If the masses were to protect their interests in a democratic fashion they had to become more articulate politically, their numbers and their methods of influencing representatives in the normal course of politics had to be increased. The political power of the entrepreneurial class had to be at least balanced by the laboring forces. To this end, therefore, demands for women's suffrage began to be made. Direct election of United States Senators was urged as being more in keeping with the democratic theme of the Constitution. There was talk of giving the people a greater share in the nomination of presidential candidates through primaries in the respective states which would permit ordinary voters to express their preferences among leading contenders. Novel proposals were made for additional processes which would permit the average voters to by-pass their representatives or check them in policy formulation. The "initiative," whereby through petition and special election the voters could enact policy independently of the legislature, was one. The "referendum," which would permit the electorate at large to halt the enactment of policies by legislative bodies, was another. Still a third was the "recall," an electoral process which would enable voters to remove an elected official from office prior to the normal expiration of his term. While not unanimously supported by the American people, all of these ideas relating to direct democracy have, to one extent or another, been incorporated in our political practices, and they have served to enhance the potentialities of the people for expressing discontent with existing policies and for choosing public officials who may best represent the viewpoints being expressed.

One further facet of the progressive period should be noted. Perhaps it was merely coincidental that this development occurred during the progressive era; more likely the nature of the atmosphere helped to shape the development. The institution of the presidency was modified in the direction of strengthened leadership and the expectation of such leadership by the people. This concept of the "strong President" had roots deep in the American past. Jefferson, Jackson, and Lincoln had all left their imprints on the office and its power potential. War and other crises had inevitably vested greater authority in the chief executive because of the necessity for leadership in the emergencies. But still, the original concept of the presidential office as being relatively weak, and even subservient to the Congress persisted. Theodore Roosevelt and Woodrow Wilson changed that for good. Roosevelt's "stewardship" theory of the presidency proclaimed that the President's prerogatives in the exercise of power in the interest of the people should not be limited to the *authorizations* prescribed in Article II of the Constitution. Rather, Roosevelt insisted, the President should take any action for the good of the people and the country not *proscribed* by Article II. The President—as steward of the people—had a responsibility to lead without too much concern for discovering adequate legal basis for his action. Wilson, while perhaps not quite as free and easy in his approach to presidential authority, certainly subscribed to the leadership principle enunciated by Roosevelt and proved it by the legislative leadership he exerted especially during his first term in office. The concept of presidential leadership which was crystallized during the progressive era has become an accepted part of American political thought, though every succeeding President has not chosen to exercise this leadership to the same extent.

The practical program of the progressives was fostered by a number of prominent political figures and was achieved to a considerable degree. Generally, economic planning and governmentally imposed restraints characterized these programs as a means of removing special privileges and more nearly equalizing the rights of all. William Jennings Bryan, for example, urged a lowered tariff, regulation or destruction of monopoly, bimetallism, a graduated income tax for the redistribution of wealth, direct election of Senators, arbitration of labor disputes, guarantees for bank deposits, and government ownership of the railroads. Theodore Roosevelt likewise urged strict regulation of trusts and a graduated income tax, and, in addition, supported a thorough conservation program in opposition to the unrestrained exploitation of our natural resources, legislation beneficial to labor, direct primaries, a more widespread use of the initiative, referendum, and recall, and a proposal for a review by the people of judicial decisions involving the constitutionality of social legislation. Wilson too favored control of trusts, and supported very effectively the concepts of lowered tariffs and banking and currency reforms.

The success of the progressives cannot be measured exclusively by the degree to which they secured their specific goals. The legacy of thought and spirit which they bequeathed to their heirs must also be weighed. But even in terms of distinct aims progressivism produced a rather enviable record. Direct election of Senators and women's suffrage became part of our constitutional system. An income tax—for better or worse—was enacted. Some degree of monopoly regulation was achieved through the Clayton Act. The Federal Reserve System revamped our banking practices. Tariffs were lowered at Wilson's urging. Roosevelt's efforts at conservation bore fruit. The initiative, referendum, and recall found their way into use in many states and localities—though not at the national level. Labor legislation was forthcoming, but it was many years before such laws became truly meaningful for America's labor force. In short, the progressives had not carried the day, but they had made a significant beginning for their cause.

The advent of World War I brought an end to the era as the country's concern turned naturally to the more pressing challenge. The end of that conflict saw Wilson's progressivism on the international scale strangled by a resurgence of isolation and the intransigence of the U.S. Senate in repudiating the President's efforts to have us join the League of Nations. "Normalcy" and a new prosperity followed with Harding and Coolidge, and the mass of the American people preferred to remain undisturbed in conscience and comfort over matters of social and economic unrest which still smouldered beneath the surface of tranquility which seemed to exist. The stock market crash of 1929 and the depression which followed indicated only too clearly that the progressives had been on the right track; the capitalist system—for all its virtues—was still subject to abuse and contained inherent contradictions which led periodically to the boom and bust of the business cycle. This new turn of events called for another reevaluation of the American system, another look at the social and economic forces which had to be harnessed and harmonized so as to produce a continually prosperous and happy society. Out of this new environment and analysis the "New Deal" was born.

The New Deal

The depression of the 1930's produced much more than prolonged economic misery for the United States. In addition it inaugurated a national Democratic party dominance that was to last twenty years, and, more importantly, it led to a constitutional revision of gigantic proportions. The depression was of such magnitude and intensity that novel approaches and new concepts of potential remedy seemed to be called for, as Franklin Roosevelt promised, a New Deal. As the depression hit, President Hoover moved quickly to take certain emergency measures which might halt the downward spiral of the economy or ameliorate its effects. But the impact of these efforts was not great and the economic slide continued. In view of the general economic circumstances it could hardly have been otherwise, and yet the Republican party had to pay the political price for holding the reins of government at this unfortunate time.

The presidential election of 1932 brought Franklin D. Roosevelt to the top office in the land and produced Democratic majorities in both houses of Congress. Though it may be debatable, many, both in and out of government, interpreted the Democratic victory as a plea—perhaps a mandate—for the new administration to adopt the necessary measures which would insure rapid recovery. With the President playing the role of leadership to the hilt, the first hundred days of the Roosevelt era saw the translation of the New Deal promises into a multitude of legislative bills, most of which received ready congressional approval. But the whole concept of the New Deal and the specific measures of which it was composed rested on a questionable base, and the fate of the initial legislative enactments describes the dilemma most accurately.

The nature of the economic crisis, since it pervaded the entire nation, called for action which was national in scope. But the areas of greatest difficulty—the decline of industrial production and the chaotic circumstances in agriculture—demanded action which was *not within the traditional sphere of jurisdiction accorded to Congress by the national Constitution.* As previously interpreted by the Supreme Court and as generally accepted in the minds of the American people, manufacturing and agriculture were activities the regulation of which remained in the hands of the individual states. Thus, while the need for action was great and pressing, the constitutional propriety of congressional actions in these spheres remained highly questionable. Nevertheless, faced with the dire necessity of the moment, both the President and Congress sought to devise ways—discover "constitutional pegs"—which would permit national action to lead the way out of the depression.

What followed in terms of policy decisions has often been called the "Roosevelt revolution"—a totally new and startling approach to interpretation of the American Constitution and the authority which it vests in the national government. To refer to this era as "revolutionary" is, I believe, misleading if not inaccurate. That document which was drafted in 1787 by men of good will, intelligence, and foresight was nevertheless a result of a number of compromises made by practical politicians in order to satisfy the conflicting interests represented by the delegates to the Philadelphia convention. It is a product of its times. Its phrases are in many cases ambiguous and consciously so to avoid further controversy in seeking its ratification. It is a document which cries for interpretation. And that interpretation began early—by the President, by Congress, and by the Supreme Court. Early interpretations by the Court under John Marshall tended to strengthen national authority and to broaden the narrow concept of "delegated" powers in the national government to include such powers as could be legitimately "implied" from the delegated powers (McCulloch *v.* Maryland). Though this tendency did not continue incessantly, through the years— as our national life evolved—there has been an over-all leaning to an enhanced authority for the federal government and a loose interpretation of the original document to that end. In view of our various national emergencies and the more closely knit relationships among the states in the federal system, such development was inevitable. But the point is that the "revolutionary" problem of constitutional justification facing the Congress in the early 1930's was not a sharp, abrupt break with the past. It was not a complete turnabout from the moderate evolutionary progression of policy change which preceded it. The past had been full of dramatic actions and interpretations; the sum of such previous actions laid adequate groundwork for the appraisal of the New Deal leaders. Constitutionally, the situation was a natural result of the *evolutionary* process which went before.

All that made the situation "revolutionary" was that with all the loose construction of national constitutional authority—especially in the areas of taxation and commerce regulation—the "traditional" conception of division of powers still left farming and industry outside the realm of federal jurisdiction, and these were precisely the areas which required national attention. When the New Deal became ultimately a reality, all that made of it still a revolutionary upheaval was the extent to which the American people supported it—the revolution in thought which had taken place with progressivism replacing individualism as the democratic ideal—the commitment which American citizens made to the new concept and the new processes. The older individualistic beliefs had not been lost, but they had been supplanted in prominence by the broader social concept of progressivism.

There was still another evolutionary (rather than revolutionary) thread in the New Deal. The Progressive Era which preceded it both philosophically and practically signaled the change which was in the making. The era had not only been dedicated to the improvement of the lot of the masses, but it had been distinctly oriented to the viewpoint that government should play a major role in assuring such improvement. Thus the idea of governmental intervention in economic affairs was similarly a part of the tide of American tradition which culminated in the New Deal. The evolution was continuing, and it was continuing in the mainstream of American thought which had been more and more accepted during the preceding two decades. The constitutional obstacles of federalism were present as bars to federal action only to the extent that they had been established by Supreme Court precedents of the past—precedents established in a different social and economic environment and subject to reconsideration in terms of the changed economic and social circumstances of the second quarter of the twentieth century.

The New Deal attacked the problems of the depression on

several fronts.[1] First there was an attempt to bolster prices. The dollar was devaluated and gold was purchased from abroad. Production limits were placed on agricultural products, petroleum, and coal. Industry was regulated with "codes of fair competition" so as to modify or eliminate some of the abuses which had crept into business methods. Additionally for agriculture loans and subsidies were utilized to supplement production control.

Secondly, private debt reduction was sought in various ways. Raising prices was one method of achieving this end, and summarily writing down the face value of debts was another. Further, new federal lending agencies were created to "guarantee" debts incurred at reasonable rates, and bankruptcy laws were revised to ease the settlement of insolvency.

While debt reduction was important, the revival and expansion of credit was even more so if economic activity was to be rejuvenated. "Pump priming" of one sort or another was a necessity in view of the reluctance or inability of the normal commercial agencies to invest in the expansion of industry during the time of trial and uncertainty. The powers and operations of the Reconstruction Finance Corporation were expanded to make loans to private businesses and public corporations in various endeavors. The Federal Reserve System was utilized to expand (or contract) credit, to govern the minimum legal reserves required of member banks (thereby affecting commercial credit), and to control the margin requirements for stock purchases thus affecting the credit of brokers' loans. Needless to say, this concept of "pump priming" was a corollary to "deficit financing" in that the national debt grew as government loaned, granted, and appropriated funds in a furious effort to bolster the economy. This path was viewed with misgivings by some but defended by others on the ground that a revivified economy would more than repay the debt through increased tax revenues. Though

[1] The following summary is found in Louis M. Hacker, "The Third American Revolution," in *The New Deal—Revolution or Evolution* (Boston: D. C. Heath, 1949), pp. 4-6.

the initial intent of these various maneuvers was to expand credit and commercial activity, the processes established permitted—in the long run—governmental supervision of credit if the aim was contraction rather than expansion.

The position of labor, not only for itself but in terms of its purchasing power, was another problem facing the New Deal. Wages were low and falling; sweatshop conditions of employment prevailed in some areas; child labor was on the increase. If labor was to be revitalized and its consuming power increased as a spur to production, various steps had to be taken. The concepts which went into New Deal planning on these matters were not novel except to the extent that the *national* government was attempting the required legislation. Minimum wage and maximum hours laws were devised; child labor was attacked; the rights of unionization and collective bargaining were legislatively recognized; the closed shop was approved. In essence, the National Labor Relations Act of 1935 (the Wagner Act), and the Fair Labor Standards Act of 1938—both held constitutional by the Supreme Court—encompassed the basic labor objectives of the New Deal.

In both immediate and long-range terms the depression emphasized the problems of the needy, the dependent, the invalid, the unemployed. The New Deal had to move speedily to alleviate existing economic distress, but it also concerned itself with more far reaching plans for the avoidance of its repetition. In the former category the Public Works Administration was established to lend money for the construction of major public facilities; under the Works Progress Administration short-term projects made work for the unemployed; and federal loans were made to the states for direct relief activities. In the latter category a long-range program of "social security" was devised and legislated. Under a grant-in-aid system, by virtue of which the national government extended financial aid which the states matched, the aged, the blind, dependent children, and the permanently disabled were assured continued monetary assistance. Unemployment compensation programs were instituted (at federal urging) in the various states and a system of public employment offices created. An Old Age and Survivors Insurance project was launched requiring employers and employees to contribute to a federal fund from which benefits could be drawn by retired workers.

Additional activities were undertaken and plans made for the reinvigoration of other aspects of the economy or for the future protection of various segments of the population. One need, for example, was the building of relatively decent residences for low-income families. To this end there was created the United States Housing Authority to provide financial assistance to public authorities in erecting such low-cost housing. For those persons with money to save or invest there had to be restored the confidence which had been shaken by the stock market crash and the closing or failure of many banks. Two agencies were established to accomplish this objective. First, the Securities and Exchange Commission was given supervisory powers over the issuance of new corporate securities and over the transactions of brokers and security exchanges. Second, the Federal Deposit Insurance Corporation was created to guarantee savings deposits up to $5,000 (since increased to $10,000).

In the area of electric power, the New Deal established what was to become one of the more controversial of its instrumentalities, the Tennessee Valley Authority. The TVA was to be a multipurpose government corporation related to national defense, interstate river development, recreation, and extension of electrical power and facilities over several states. Though at first opposed by the private power interests, the TVA was justified not only in terms of the national interest, but on the grounds that private power companies were either unable or unwilling to provide the necessary capital outlay for the creation of such a gigantic enterprise. While still not universally applauded, the operations of TVA have come to be generally accepted by the American public as making a significant contribution in its various objectives to the inhabitants of the areas in which it operates and to the general welfare of the nation.

And finally, the national administration concerned itself with the revival of foreign trade. In order for a country like the United States to expand successfully its productive activities with its concomitant rise in employment and purchasing power it must be able to engage in a fairly lively foreign exchange. Such exchange is, of course, a two-way street, but one which tends to benefit most the kind of industrialized economy possessed by the United States. In order to stimulate such trade, however, special enticements had to be provided in the circumstances which prevailed. Two principal steps were taken during the New Deal to provide such motivation. On the one hand, the Export-Import Bank was established to extend credits to foreign governments and to stimulate the flow of goods. On the other, Congress was convinced to authorize the drafting of a number of reciprocal trade agreements with other countries, having the net effect of lowering American tariffs on a variety of goods, thus making it easier for foreign nations to trade with the United States.

In sum then, the Roosevelt administration surveyed the entire spectrum of economic activity in this country and abroad bearing on the American depression and undertook a wide variety of steps designed to ameliorate existing conditions, stimulate the economic process, and provide safeguards against a recurrence of the circumstances which had fostered the depression. Needless to say, in the press of the emergency, measures were hastily—and not too carefully—drawn, they were rushed into execution, they were not totally successful, and, in some cases at least, they were of doubtful constitutionality. The major difficulty facing the New Deal analysts and legislators was, as previously stated, that those areas of economic activity which were in greatest need of "treatment" were areas which had traditionally been considered to be within the realm of state jurisdiction and beyond the scope of federal authority. Yet the states seemed to be incapable of acting either individually or collectively to remedy the economic malady with which they were faced. Thus it became necessary for the national government to attempt to discern constitutional bases on which to found the legitimacy of the legislation designed to bring the country out of the depression. The bases which suggested themselves and which were utilized for the onslaught on poverty, misery, and economic chaos were the taxing and spending powers and the power to regulate interstate commerce.

Despite the exigencies of the time the force of tradition and precedent was strong, and the concept of economic laissez-faire as well as the limitations inherent in the federal system were predominant in the thoughts of the members of the Supreme Court who were called upon to rule on the constitutionality of early New Deal legislation. The fate of several of the key laws passed in the early 1930's was indicative of the prevailing sentiment among the jurists as well as a sizeable segment of public opinion. The validity of the National Industrial Recovery Act providing codes of fair competition for industry was questioned in the case of Schechter Poultry Co. *v.* United States (295 U.S. 495). In addition to the fact that the Court unanimously considered the law to establish an illegal delegation of legislative power to the President, the supreme judicial body also assessed the act as a federal invasion of an area traditionally reserved to state authority. In United States *v.* Butler (297 U.S. 1) the first Agricultural Adjustment Act which sought to regulate agricultural production and to finance the program through a tax on the processors of farm products was cut down by the Supreme Court as an illegal invasion of state authority and an unconstitutional use of the taxing power. The Court's reaction to New Deal legislation provoked a "great debate" in the United States and culminated in a presidentially sponsored plan to "pack" the Court in order to override the conservative votes of the elderly judges—a plan which was rejected by the Congress.

Nevertheless, the New Deal philosophy was to triumph. Resignations on the Supreme Court permitted the President to make new appointments of more liberally oriented justices, and new —and more carefully drawn—laws were prepared to accomplish the objectives sought by the administration. Once again it was the power to regulate interstate commerce which was used as the basis for federal intervention, and this time the attempt was successful. In 1937, in National Labor Relations Board *v.* Jones and Laughlin Steel Corporation (301 U.S. 1) the Court held the Wagner Act applicable to the labor-management relations of the manufacturing concern on the grounds that, though primarily a fabricating establishment, Jones and Laughlin's activities had a sufficient impact on commerce as to warrant the application of the act as a proper congressional prerogative. This decision, of course, was a significant deviation from the traditional proposition that manufacturing was *not* commerce and was thus beyond congressional jurisdiction. This concept of the interrelationship between production and commerce was reinforced in 1939 in Mulford *v.* Smith (307 U.S. 38). In this case the Agricultural Adjustment Act of 1938 which set production quotas for certain agricultural products was held constitutional as a legitimate exercise of the commerce power of Congress. Still another landmark case was that of United States *v.* Darby Lumber Co. (312 U.S. 100) which, in 1941, upheld the validity of national regulation of wages, hours, and child labor for a large segment of American industry.

The New Deal maneuvers and the Supreme Court decisions which finally upheld their constitutionality were not given universal accolade by the American people. Many Americans were concerned with results, naturally, not with constitutional niceties. Some did not understand the constitutional issues. Still others, even though they may have felt the necessity for federal action, were concerned with the implications of the novel constitutional interpretations by virtue of which the national administration was now active in fields which had long been considered as reserved to state discretion. Perhaps the most accurate assessment of the 1930 developments is that, while they stemmed from the pressing necessity of the economic emergency, they represented a fairly realistic approach to the solution of problems in terms of the changed nature of the American economic system itself. Although it is true that "manufacturing" and "commerce" are not necessarily one and the same thing and that they may exist separately and distinctly from each other, by 1930 the small manufacturer, the tiny industry, the little entrepreneur had been replaced to a large extent by the giant corporation whose distribution apparatus could not be effectively distinguished from its manufacturing enterprise. Business had become a mixture of making and selling which brought it within the field of congressional regulation.

The Mixed Economy

The Progressive Era and the New Deal created a climate of opinion and an organizational pattern of governmental supervision of and even participation in the economy of the United States. Prompted by ideological considerations—partly of socialist orientation, and motivated more directly by the exigencies of the great depression these two movements modified significantly the concept and practices of economic laissez-faire. But the movements did not initiate the modifications. The roots of such developments lay deep in America's past. Rather, these movements might best be described as the culmination of drives which had begun decades earlier and were brought to fruition as much by force of circumstances as by the support which reform ideas had generated. That these 20th century practices reflected "socialist" objectives to some extent was, perhaps, incidental, and the extent to which the American "free enterprise" economy has become "socialized" must be measured in comparative terms and the history of the American economy dating back to its earliest days.

While the United States has historically been committed to free enterprise economic principles it must be recognized that our economic activities, like those of all other states, have never been totally "free." To begin with, such a "socialist" activity as the postal service, organized and implemented by the national government, has been with us from the beginning of our constitutional history. Public educational systems devised and carried out by individual state authorities have long been recognized as desirable practices in American life. But more than this, even the most outspoken defenders of economic laissez-faire have frequently sought and obtained governmental "intervention" in the free play of economic forces through such devices as protective tariffs and subsidies. Protection through the issuance of patents and copyrights were other aids to business. Such items as these, alone or in combination, would never have classified the American economy as socialistic. Such isolated instances of governmental regulation or governmental performance of functions which might have been undertaken by private enterprise were simply accepted as part of the proper role of government in a society which was dedicated to the principles of economic individualism. However, through the years many additional instances of governmental regulation and/or control made their appearance, so that by the time of the New Deal the American people were attuned to the idea of government playing at least a supervisory role in an essentially free economy.

The hierarchy of national regulatory agencies had its beginning in 1887 with the establishment of the Interstate Commerce Commission to regulate rates and supervise the business practices of railroads. Subsequently its jurisdiction was extended to certain aspects of motor and water transportation as well as the shipment of petroleum through pipelines. By 1890 the minimizing of competition between large corporation through the creation of "trusts" had generated a sufficiently large popular demand that Congress responded with the passage of the Sherman Antitrust Act designed to prevent monopolistic business practices. In 1914 the Clayton Act was passed to clarify and strengthen the original effort. These early regulatory measures—preceded in many instances by state restraints on business activity—ultimately blossomed into a considerable number of "independent" boards and commissions to oversee and/or control various aspects of the economy.

In 1914 the Federal Trade Commission was created to prohibit unfair methods of competition. Even before that (1906) the national government had sought to protect the public against impure food and drugs vesting the enforcement of the protective legislation in various governmental bodies. In 1920 the Federal Power Commission was established to survey the country's water resources and approve power projects. Today the Commission not only has broad powers in connection with hydroelectric activities but has some authority over the interstate sale of natural gas. The Federal Communications Commission dates from 1934 and has significant regulatory functions in the fields of telephone and telegraph facilities and radio and television. Since 1938 the Civil Aeronautics Board and the Civil Aeronautics Administration have cooperated in such things as the certification of planes and pilots, the promulgation of safety regulations, and the issuance of licenses to improve the safety and comfort of air travel. These and other agencies have come into being usually to meet some new need growing out of technical advances or to provide a needed curtailment of some abuse of free enterprise which for some reason could not be done effectively by state authority. It is important to keep in mind, however, that though regulation, supervision, or control was initiated in these various areas, those essential elements of a laissez-faire economy—private ownership and the opportunity to make fair profits through fair competition which was not injurious to the general interest —remained unimpaired.

To be sure there have been, in addition to those examples already noted, numerous instances of direct government participation in economic enterprise at the national, state, and local levels. In addition to TVA, for instance, the national government owns and operates the Bonneville Dam, the Grand Coulee Dam, and something over 150 hydroelectric and steam generating plants. The government corporations began to flourish at the time of World War I and mushroomed during the depression when many new corporations were created especially for lending purposes. Though there has been a significant reduction in their number, there remain such examples as the Federal Deposit Insurance Corporation, the Virgin Islands Corporation, the

Saint Lawrence Seaway Development Corporation, and the Panama Canal Company, over and above the corporate activities in the areas of water and electricity. Further, local governments have been active participants as owners and operators of economic enterprises. Waterworks, transportation facilities, power and light services—public utilities generally—have been and still are owned by many municipalities or other local governmental agencies. Many recreational facilities are state enterprises. In some states, the distribution of alcoholic beverages is a state monopoly. Toll roads, port facilities, warehouses, and grain elevators are among other examples of direct state participation in economic affairs. In short, there is no question that we have had and continue to have in the United States a considerable amount of governmental ownership and operation of business enterprises at all levels.

Since, by definition, socialism by and large has called for government ownership and operation of sizeable segments of the economy, and since in the United States the Socialist party has sought such limited objectives as minimum wage and maximum hour legislation which have been obtained, the question which suggests itself is, "Do the developments described above, culminating in the welfare state, make the American economy 'socialistic?'" Or, at the very least, can it be said that the American economy by virtue of these developments has moved closer to socialism? Superficially, the natural tendency might be to answer one or the other of these questions in the affirmative. After all, there are striking coincidences of objective and attainment between American socialists and New Dealers. And certainly the array of government economic enterprises coincides with socialist desires for public ownership and operation. However, a deeper analysis of the American economic system in the 1960's might give a more qualified answer, if not a totally different one.

It must be kept in mind that "socialism," "communism," "capitalism," or "New Dealism" are terms used to describe relatively complex *systems* and the *aggregate* of ideas and concepts which they encompass. There is too frequently the temptation to generalize too readily from too limited evidence. Policies, practices, and ideology must be evaluated in their totality to arrive at sound conclusions. Individual and isolated characteristics may be deceptive and misleading. Instances of governmental ownership of certain production facilities do *not*, of and by themselves, prove conclusively the existence of a socialist society. Controls and planning applied to the economic system by government may, on further investigation, be shown to be compatible with a basically capitalist economy.

The key question in a systematic appraisal of any "ism" must surely be: "What are its determining attributes?" In capitalism, a prime attribute is private ownership of the means of production. A second is the opportunity to derive fair profit from the use of one's resources or the application of one's energy. A third is the freedom to make economic decisions relatively independently. And a fourth is the tacit approval of the virtues seemingly inherent in the system—the promotion of free competition, initiative, ingenuity, and hard work. In short, capitalism implies the freedom of the individual to pursue his economic endeavors under a profit motive with a minimum of governmental control *consistent with the public well being*. It should be noted that capitalism as an economic system is not descriptive of practices and processes alone, but of attitudes, outlooks, and approaches which relate to and fashion the context within which the practices occur.

In socialism the emphasis is reversed. Private ownership, though permitted in wide sections of the economy, is considered potentially or inherently evil and the basis for the exploitation of the many by the few. The profit motive is held to be inimical to the public welfare. Government planning and operation supersede and seriously curtail individual enterprise in many fields. Cooperation for the public good is claimed to be superior to competition as the best path to the attainment of the economic well being of the greater segment of society. In other words, not only the economic organization of society is altered under socialism but its orientation in thought as well.

In this writer's opinion, therefore, the contention that the United States has, in the last three decades, become socialistic is not tenable. The essential premises of a capitalist society have not been undermined by those developments epitomized in the New Deal. Private ownership of productive facilities remains the rule. The making of profits is not demeaned, and the American business community in the mid-1960's continues to announce the largest profits in history despite heavy tax schedules. Government owned and operated economic enterprises at all levels comprise only a very small section of total economic activity and would be considered too few in number to satisfy most orthodox socialists. And the pattern of government regulatory machinery and practice, though extensive and easily thought of as onerous by the individual businessman, still permits a wide latitude for freedom of choice and action by American industry, farmers, distributors, and consumers. It might be added that, in comparison with the amount of governmental enterprise and range of control in other countries, governmental restraint on the American free economy remains relatively mild.

Obviously this opinion is not universally held and is legitimately subject to challenge. The difficulty of arriving at a consensus in this area stems not only from personal differences in economic status and philosophy, but from differences of interpretation as to what circumstances in a capitalist operation require governmental intervention *in the public interest* and to what extent such intervention should take place. While some spokesmen and publicists minimize their importance, certain facts cannot be denied. Some individuals and groups did abuse the privileges of free enterprise; economic liberty was, at least occasionally, interpreted as license to exploit. Monopolies and trusts were formed to moderate or eliminate competition. Low wages, long hours, and poor working conditions did exist for many in the United States at the same time that fortunes were being built by a comparative few. Even without the presence of abuses, the unplanned and even chaotic nature of capitalist decision-making seemed destined to produce periodically the boom and bust of the business cycle despite the best good will of individual entrepreneurs. At what point in this whole developmental process the *public interest* became sufficiently involved as to warrant governmental action presumably will always be debated. Whether the amount of intervention has been too great or too little will likewise remain an unresolved question. And whether government planning and regulation should have been basically localized or centralized in the national regime continues as a subject of heated discussion.

Even when the concession is made that the United States of today is not really socialistic, it may be described as "leaning towards socialism," "subject to creeping socialism," or "drifting into socialism," because of the broadening of governmental regulation since the 1930's. Again on the surface this may appear logical, and there is no denying the broad acceptance of governmental supervision of the economy by the American people. Government, for the most part, is no longer feared; it is looked on as friend and benefactor by the greater portion of the American society. And, in this vein, Americans could be more prepared psychologically to accept greater governmental participation in the economy.

But there is another side to this coin. The argument can be made that the developments of the last thirty years *have made the potentiality of real socialism less likely* in America. The reasoning is simple. The American economic tradition is capitalistic. Its existence and accomplishment contributed significantly to America's high living standards. Americans were not likely to discard lightly familiar practices and cherished optimism. But as abuses in the system became more flagrant, as dreams of ascending the economic ladder remained unfulfilled for increasing numbers of persons, as economic conditions remained static or grew worse instead of better, as the opportunities of the geographic and economic frontier dwindled, and as the misery of periodic economic depression became more acute, the attractiveness of capitalism became tarnished and the appeal of such systems as socialism and communism grew for tens of thousands of American industrial and farm laborers. Fortunately, the path of remedy and amelioration which was followed—laborer and farmer organization and protest, the petitioning of government for restraint of abuse, the seeking for greater order in economic activity, the development under governmental auspices of positive conditions for full development of the citizen and his protection in old age and infirmity—*remained firmly within capitalist ideology.* All of the remedial action *accepted the essential premises of capitalist economics.* Only the undesirable in the system —stemming from personal greed or inherent weakness—was modified. In these circumstances, then, the typical American, more economically secure, more aware of the advantages of the capitalist system—moderately restrained—for all, more confident in the entrepreneur and his government, more optimistic about the future, became *less likely to accept the appeals of an alien ideology* which gave no indication of surpassing that status which he had achieved.

Whatever may be the most apt opinion on these matters or the most precise phrase to describe what has occurred, this much seems clear. Today the United States has a mixed economy in which private enterprise in greater proportion and governmental enterprise and regulation in lesser proportion exist side by side. The standard of capitalism continues to fly strongly, and the basic virtues and practices of free enterprise continue to make important practical and ideological contributions. To the extent that laissez-faire has been modified, it must be conceded that the various socialist movements in this country had a significant influence. The American economy may be far from perfect, but it is certainly superior in the eyes of the majority of American citizens—whatever it may be called. What is perhaps most important to remember in self-assessment is that personal interest normally makes objective consideration difficult, and that the resort to overly generalized words and phrases as epithets not only clouds facts and issues through misunderstanding but generates emotional turmoil which further adds to the difficulty. To expect a complete elimination of prejudice or to hope for an exclusion of economic prejudice from the inescapable exaggeration of partisan politics may be asking too much. To urge an *effort* at greater rationality in economic, social, and political matters is, I believe, the proper plea for continuing advance.

STUDY QUESTIONS AND PROJECT SUGGESTIONS

1. A. Discuss the general nature of the "progressive era" in the United States.
   B. Outline the specific political and economic objectives of the progressives and indicate the extent to which their goals were attained.

2. Evaluate "muckraking" and "iconoclasm" as techniques of social and economic reform.

3. Write a brief essay on the topic: "The New Deal did not constitute a revolution in American political and economic ideology."

4. Why did initial New Deal legislation fail to get judicial approval, and how was this obstacle ultimately overcome?

5. Outline the major steps taken by Franklin Roosevelt's administration to combat the effects of the depression of the 1930's.

6. Describe the major features of the "welfare state."

7. Explain how the advent of the American "welfare state" may have prevented the development of a more socialistic economy.

CHAPTER 10

MODERN BRITISH SOCIALISM

With Great Britain's long existence as a nation-state, its leadership in the industrial revolution, its insular situation, and its long history of socialist orientation, it is not surprising to find in the contemporary British economy a considerable degree of socialist organization and practice. The Fabian Society's influence has, of course, been strong, and the British Labor party has served as the principal vehicle for socialist political action. But in Great Britain as in so many other states—the march to socialism, or partial socialism, has been the product of many factors in the economic and social realms, with the Conservative party responding to various circumstances in much the same fashion as Labor later did. Though the degree of "socialism" in Great Britain is considerably higher than that in the United States, the British themselves—with the exception of some Labor party members, tend to describe their economic arrangements as constituting a "welfare state."

The British welfare state has many of the same objectives and some of the same practices as did the American New Deal, though in the British case they have been more widespread, practiced with a greater intensity, and composed of certain techniques which, for the most part, have been absent from the American program. The absence of judicial review from the English political system may also have made economic developments simpler as no judicial confirmation of parliamentary action was necessary. In terms of objectives, the British goals are not unlike those of most nations in this highly complex modern world in which the spread of political democracy has been accompanied by demands for greater economic equality and opportunity. Thus the British have sought full employment (the influence of John M. Keynes being notable here) and a society all of whose members, even those unemployable, might enjoy a standard of living which though minimal is adequate. To accomplish this end, British leaders have recognized that there must be high productivity, financial stability, and a favorable international trade environment since Great Britain depends so much on imports and exports. As to techniques, the British picture is not significantly different from that in other quarters of the world. Economic planning and regulation are an integral part of the process. A redistribution of wealth, designed not merely to improve the lot of the masses but to broaden the consuming base of the economy, has been accomplished by revising tax laws and schedules and by various social security laws. And nationalization of privately owned industries has occurred to bring them under the direct jurisdiction of the state.

This development of the welfare state has been particularly noticeable since World War II, but, as in the case of the United States, its origins must be traced back to the 19th century. As early as 1802 Great Britain's extended experience with the industrial revolution and laissez-faire capitalism had produced demands for reform, and certain Factory Acts were passed relating to maximum hours of employment in designated enterprises and regulating the conditions of employment of women and children. Subsequently there were enacted Poor Laws (1834), public health measures (1848), and laws providing for public elementary education (1870). The latter part of the century also witnessed developments which were to have repercussions for the future: the growth and legal recognition of trade unionism and the beginnings of an extended franchise to workers.

It should be noted further that though modern British socialistic ideology had not yet made its appearance, early in the 19th century, the prevailing economic philosophy was one of some kinship. In the 18th century Adam Smith's economic individualism and Edmund Burke's political conservatism may have dominated, but by the 19th they were essentially replaced by the utilitarianism of Jeremy Bentham. According to the utilitarians, the criterion of effective society and government was whether they produced "the greatest good for the greatest number," and, to the extent that this ideal was missing, Parliament should act positively to remedy the situation. This was hardly the concept of laissez-faire. Oddly enough, the utilitarians did not levy as heavy an attack as they might have on capitalist economics, because their concept of affirmative parliamentary action ran afoul of the practical existence of protective tariffs—legislatively enacted—on grain, a situation which hurt the many rather than the few. Therefore, since they sought the abolition or lowering of such tariffs, the utilitarians made a polite bow in the direction of free trade. Nevertheless, there was no question that the dominant theme of governmental intervention in society's affairs for the good of most persons was what the utilitarians advocated. Additionally, the utilitarians trained their guns specifically on a number of their society's culprits, notably the criminal code and penal institutional practices, and succeeded in achieving needed reforms. In so doing, they established firmly the precedent of remedy for abuse through state action.

Against this background of philosophy and practice the turn into the 20th century saw the groundwork laid for the later nationalization measures. This was accomplished by the creation of several corporations and agencies which brought government into the economic arena as a direct participant. In 1900, for example, the Liberal party majority created the Port of London

Authority with operational jurisdiction over docks and harbor facilities. In 1926 the Conservatives followed this line with the establishment of the Central Electricity Board, and continued with the chartering of the British Broadcasting Corporation (1927) and the creation of the London Passenger Transport Board (1933). (Even the post-World War II nationalization activities undertaken by the Labor party, it should be noted, were undertaken as the result of recommendations made by investigating committees dominated by Conservatives.)

When British socialism came to full flowering then in the years after the Second World War, it represented, perhaps even more strongly than developments in the United States, a continuing evolution of the economic climate rather than an abrupt change of direction. The seeds of nationalization had been sown earlier, and there remained only to tend them to maturity. Again perhaps more markedly than in the American experience the most recent evolutionary stage of economic organization represents a reaction to force of circumstance at least as much—if not more —than it does a response to ideological motivation, though there was a striking consensus among the British as to the best postwar course. Before examining in greater detail the nature of the contemporary economy of Great Britain, it might be well to scrutinize more closely those forces which pointed to modern practice.

To begin with, Great Britain's geographic situation presents certain inherent problems. International trade is a matter of life and death to the English; possessing limited resources, foodstuffs and other raw materials must be imported to feed people and machines, and manufactured goods must be marketed consistently to insure a reasonably favorable trade balance. The British economy also depends in large measure on certain "intangible" revenues, such as those derived from shipping. Long before World War II the British position had been deteriorating as the result of the competition from other developing industrial powers both on the continent and elsewhere, and the Great Depression worsened an already bad situation.

A second—and somewhat surprising—contributing factor in Britain's economic evolution is its long experience in industrialization.[1] It might legitimately be assumed that Great Britain's leadership in the industrial revolution would give it perennially an advantage in the international competition in production and marketing of goods. Instead, however, the reverse seems to be the case. Once English factories had established their pattern of machine production it was not always economically practicable to incorporate the latest technical advances into the existing context of capital equipment. It was more economically feasible to repair existing machinery, which though less efficient retained considerable productive life, than it was to retool completely. On the other hand, nations newly come to the period of industrialization were likely to make use of the most advanced and efficient machinery. When one adds to this the pressures of belligerency in two World Wars it is easy to see that much of British industrial capacity is old, outmoded, even obsolete and yet not easy to replace on economic or psychological grounds. Thus British longevity in the period of industrial revolution turns out to be a burden rather than a boon.

The most far-reaching effect on the English economy, of course, was the impact of World War II. The continuing state of emergency made almost impossible demands on Britain's productive facilities and contributed in large measure to the deterioration of its industrial plant. The need to purchase war material had the dual effect of raising the national debt tremendously and leading to the liquidation of over a billion pounds of foreign investment. At the same time, the physical destruction of capital facilities and personal property which had to be replaced after victory left Great Britain in an almost insoluble economic dilemma. Even with the prospect of American economic assistance the outlook was not bright.

Given the nature and intensity of the problem—the depletion

---

[1] See the suggestion in Samuel H. Beer and Adam B. Ulam (eds.), *Patterns of Government* (2nd ed., New York: Random House, 1962), p. 204.

and destruction of economic resources, the pressing and competing demands to which the economy had to respond when hostilities ended, the importance of international trade to Britain's national life—could British leaders conscientiously avoid a resort to controls, planning, or even nationalization of industry in the search for a sound base from which to begin the slow climb to economic recovery? Could they permit the freedom of choice and activity so characteristic of free enterprise in the face of existing circumstances? Must not a centralized direction of economic activity have appeared as the only rational approach to the solution of the problems with which Great Britain was confronted? Thus when the Labor party gained a parliamentary majority in 1945 they were impelled to follow the course which they did not only philosophically but pragmatically. Nor were the Conservatives particularly strong objectors. The organization for war, all other factors aside, had accustomed the British people to broad governmental direction, and all sectors of the population seemed to accept as "natural" a continuation of this same legislative and administrative direction to meet the "crisis" of peace.

The characteristics of the welfare state which evolved in postwar England can be easily misunderstood or distorted by those who fail to recognize (or consciously disregard) the historical events moulding it or the principal economic theory guiding it. While the British Labor party had a distinct socialist orientation and did indulge in nationalization, the overall economic principles coloring the total program were Keynesian rather than socialist. John M. Keynes was concerned with the shortcomings of capitalism, but he was not a socialist. Instead, like many others, Keynes recognized that the free market economy, left to itself, could not be relied upon to provide consistently the optimum economic advantages for the whole society. Still he saw the virtues of the system which he desired to preserve. Thus the trick was to retain free enterprise with enough guidance to avoid the abuses and maladies to which it was subject. For Keynes this could be accomplished best by "indirect" governmental action rather than such direct activities as rationing, price and wage controls, licensing, and allocation of scarce resources by administrative fiat. Indirect action involved primarily fiscal policies—control of interest rates, taxation, government expenditures, and others. The chief objective to be sought was full employment, and this, Keynes thought, could be best achieved by a judicious use of the government's spending power. Therefore, it should be kept in mind that though direct controls and nationalization have been parts of the economic picture, the moderation of the Keynesian position has been a central theme in Britain's total scheme of economic planning.

Nationalization of industry was far more limited than generally realized, and where it occurred it was characterized by a seemingly pressing need for such nationalization and by a generous compensation for the private owners whose property was taken. What constitutes a "pressing need" for the transfer of property from private to public hands is a debatable issue. But the Laborites at least set forth certain criteria as guidelines to nationalization. If an industry was monopolistic, inefficient, too small for economical functioning, a basic supplier of raw materials, or suffering from poor labor-management relations, it was a potential object of national expropriation. On this basis the Bank of England, coal, gas, electricity, some aspects of inland transportation, air transport, wireless communications, and iron and steel were nationalized, and, of course, medical services in a limited way—an important but still relatively small portion of the total economy.

The specific reasons for the nationalization of the Bank of England and the coal industry are still more illustrative.[2] In the case of the Bank, its relations with the Treasury were so close that it was almost a government entity, and its functions were such that the government wished to insure that it could be used without question as a tool of economic planning and fiscal policy.

[2] *Ibid.*, pp. 210-211.

The coal situation was even more typical. Coal had been an especially vital item in the industrial life of the country, but by 1945 the industry was beset by a number of ills. It was poorly organized and backward technically; working conditions were bad and accident rates were high; though profits continued to be made, they were made at the cost of low wages, long hours and skimping on maintenance expenditures; capital was not being enticed into the industry despite the profits and the importance of the industry; industrial relations were, to say the least, unsatisfactory. Several investigating commissions had reported the weaknesses and recommended changes, but nothing tried seemed to remedy the situation. Nationalization was the only course as far as the Laborites were concerned.

The pragmatic rather than ideological motives behind the nationalization movement were observable in the other nationalization measures, and still more in the kind of industrial organization which followed nationalization. There was no wholesale reshuffling of personnel, no downgrading or removal of key managerial individuals, no transference of decision-making to the workers themselves except at the very lowest levels of employment. The aims of syndicalism were not the objectives of nationalization. Rather the pattern of management remained similar to that before nationalization as ways were sought to improve productive efficiency and the general working conditions in the nationalized industries.

Turning to economic planning, note should be made of the techniques which have been utilized to attain the goals which were so important. In the matter of full employment, the Keynesian suggestion of government spending has been followed, and it was bolstered by some government direction of the location of industry. A 1945 act brought the Board of Trade in as an adviser on the location of new plants, and licensing requirements for new industrial construction more directly assured that industrial potential would be located in those areas where labor was available but unemployed, rather than in spots where unemployment was no particular problem. The aim of full employment was only one of several important economic objectives, however.

Maintaining a favorable balance of payments was another important goal in post-war Britain. Here, it was imperative that two correlative objectives must be attained: reduction of imports and expansion of exports. In both areas direct tactics were employed. A system of import licensing could be relied upon to control the flow of goods into England; to stimulate export, governmental "restrictions" on domestic sales suggested to manufacturers the obvious alternative of the foreign market, and high sales taxes diminished the demands for certain products at home.

While the stimulation of production was not a problem after 1945—there being such a great demand for all sorts of goods and services, insuring that available resources went into the right sort of production was. Simultaneously, care had to be taken that the economy which was so saturated with demand would not be rocked by inflation as production started to flow, an effect which would not only be dangerous in itself, but might seriously deter the export of goods abroad. The methods used to accomplish these objectives were again direct. Licensing provisions were made for the use of various scarce and important resources; government subsidies went to producers of certain goods and to those who held price levels steady; pressure from the administration for the maintenance of wage and dividend ceilings brought compliance; excess profits taxes drained away an inflationary potential; and a generally high level of income taxation had the result of reducing purchasing power especially among the higher income groups.

As production increased there was still a concern in government circles with the rate of productivity—the output per man hour of labor. Technological advances had occurred during the war years, and these were incorporated in the industrial process. But more were thought desirable. Therefore, the Labor government created a number of Working Parties—and later Development Councils—consisting of management and union representation and specialists who were to do a thorough job of research in various industrial enterprises and to come up with recommendations for improving conditions of productivity in each case examined.

British agriculture, like its industry, was in bad shape at the conclusion of hostilities, but it had been so for many years preceding World War II. In the decade before the war the Tory government had created a number of Marketing Boards with authority to subsidize and regulate the prices of British agricultural production. In 1947 a new piece of legislation established a relationship between the government and the farmer designed to induce and/or coerce the agricultural producer to farm in the most efficient manner. Briefly stated, the arrangement was that the government would guarantee prices of agricultural commodities so long as the individual farmer managed his land and crops efficiently. As the ultimate sanction, a farmer guilty of gross mismanagement could be dispossessed of his land.

While the British were refurbishing their economy in the broader sense, they, like the Americans, were concerned with the "human" element in the economy, particularly those whose status made them less practical participants in the economic process—the sick, the disabled, the aged, the unemployed. But the humanitarian element in this concern was coupled with the realization that erecting safeguards against a repetition of the devastation of the Great Depression dictated a consideration of these elements in the population, and that, ultimately, in an improving economy all segments of society should be possessed of a minimum purchasing power both for their own benefit and that of the economy. The implementation of this concern naturally involved some degree of redistribution of wealth in postwar Britain, and several techniques were brought into play.

One such technique was the enactment of various "social insurance" laws designed to assure economic protection for all citizens "from the cradle to the grave." These insurance plans were to be financed by compulsory contributions from both employees and employers and offered financial protection not

only against the aforementioned problems of unemployment, ill-
ness, and age, but for the circumstances of maternity and widow-
hood as well. In addition, special benefits were afforded for
burial expenses. It is not difficult to note a striking similarity of
both objective and process between the British and the American
systems of social security.

A second category of services was to be provided directly out
of tax revenues whose sources were primarily the more affluent
sections of English society. During the initiation of the social
insurance program and to provide for contingencies which the
social welfare plans did not cover, special kinds of public assistance were made available as direct grants. More typical and
more important are the measures allotting regular continuing
benefits either to the entire population or special categories of
persons. For example, each British family receives a "family
allowance" for each child after the first. For a time certain basic
foods were made available for children's use through local
authorities. Still another type of benefit was made available
indirectly. Government subsidies to producers, coupled in some
instances with price controls, insured moderate prices for essential food and clothes so that they could be purchased by lower
income groups. But probably the most publicized—and perhaps
misunderstood—facet of the direct, tax-financed public benefit
is the program of "socialized medicine." Because of its impact
on the British society and the interest which Americans have
shown in the program, the plan requires a bit of elaboration.

In the first place, neither the medical profession nor all medical facilities were taken over by the government. A number of
hospitals for example remained in private hands, and doctors
were free to join the program or not as they saw fit. (Most have.)
The program was to be financed from taxation and from certain
minor fees to be charged for particular services, e.g., the securing of spectacles. On the basis of the tax paid, any English
citizen was then to be entitled to any kind of medical service
which he required without additional charge. The taxes of the
healthy, of course, helped to defray the cost of treating the

infirm. As for the medical practitioners, they could remain in private practice and charge regular fees, and if patients chose to come to them and pay the fees it was their privilege. For those who chose to affiliate with the program, there was to be a flat rate of return from the government, plus an additional increment for each patient on the doctor's rolls. In short, government became the paymaster for the greater portion of the medical profession as a means of insuring adequate medical care for all citizens. It did not attempt to control further medical training, process, or ethics.

As might be expected, the plan did not work perfectly at first and it generated considerable criticism both at home and abroad. The total impact of socialism and its advantages and disadvantages will be discussed later in this work, but at this point some of the criticisms directed at Britain's national health service might be examined. Those who opposed the development raised the question of what the program would do to the initiative of the medical profession if it was deprived of its opportunity for increasing income through superior service. Would the loss of attractiveness of the profession then lead to an ultimate scarcity of doctors? Would the opportunity of the people to seek medical assistance for the slightest—even imagined—malady swamp medical facilities so that the truly ill would receive inadequate treatment? Was it proper to tax the strong for the benefit of the weak? Was the program financially sound? Would the psychological rapport between the patient and his physician break down? Would some physicians be tempted to pad their incomes by attempting to treat too many patients giving each less than the best consideration in the process?

In its initial phases the program was less than a complete success, but this should not have been unexpected since both a physical and psychological adjustment had to be made. But the charges made by the critics frequently exaggerated those problems which actually did exist. Little by little, of course, the shortcomings were remedied, and the dire consequences which had been prophecied never became a reality. Today it seems relatively certain that the program is a success.[3] The health service is widely and warmly applauded by the British people themselves. The nature of the compensation arrangements does not appear to have had an adverse effect on the number of persons entering the medical profession. There has been no lowering of the caliber of service rendered. As might well have been expected, the dedication of the medical practitioners has not been diminished; pride in the profession and the ethical standards and responsibilities which it demands precluded this from the beginning.

This appraisal of the British national health service should not be construed as a call for the adoption of a similar program in the United States. The success of an innovation in one national environment does not necessarily guarantee a similar success in another. The American system with its privately handled medical and hospital insurance plans may be superior for us. But it is important, I believe, to view developments, wherever they occur, objectively, and not to deceive ourselves through innate prejudices or mistaken beliefs.

Administration of the Nationalized Industries

The advent of the welfare state brought the need for an administrative structure to operate the nationalized industries and implement the pattern of controls and regulation which was authorized. Further, lines of supervision and responsibility had to be established between the operating agencies and the higher authority which had created them. As an answer to these needs Parliament chose the public corporation as the agency to be directly responsible for the operation of public industry.

This choice was prompted primarily by a belief that efficient management required a degree of autonomy which could be

[3] A recent visit to Great Britain by the writer tends to confirm the conclusion stated here.

achieved only outside of the normal bureaucratic hierarchy. Thus the corporate entity could conduct its affairs in an atmosphere of greater freedom than if it had been established as an arm of a particular ministry. However, the freedom was far from complete. Each corporation is supervised by a minister who is responsible to Parliament for its accomplishments. Such minister appoints and removes members of the controlling board of the corporation and is vested with certain powers of direction though the board itself is responsible for actual operation and management. In addition, the minister approves borrowing and capital investments and research programs. He also makes an annual report to Parliament. The board members are a mixture of directors of private businesses, who predominate numerically, the professional managers of the nationalized industries, and representatives of the trade unions and the cooperatives.

As Labor recognized that the policies and practices of the public corporations would come under close popular scrutiny and/or criticism they attempted to provide various agencies and lines of accountability which would minimize any attack from the beginning. One of these devices was the consumer council created in relation to each of the nationalized facilities. These councils are appointed by the appropriate minister after consultation with representative consumer groups. As a rule they also include some members of the governing boards of the corporations. There is no firm pattern of size or organization; membership ranges from three to thirty, and the councils may exist as national, regional or local entities. The consumer councils meet only infrequently—six to eight times a year, and their function is to make recommendations for the conduct of the industry from the viewpoint of the consumer. The councils have made only moderate contributions to the improvement of industrial enterprise because there has been some difficulty in getting a consensus of consumer desires and because, even when recommendations are made, their implementation is often difficult or tedious.

A much more significant control over nationalized industries, apart from that exercised by the responsible minister, is that imposed by Parliament or its individual members. While the intent in creating the semi-autonomous public corporations was to grant an additional degree of freedom, Parliament did not surrender its rights of supervision and ultimate control. The minister, being aware of his responsibility to Parliament is likely to keep a careful eye on the corporation's preceedings, but, additionally, the Parliament as a whole supervises the operations of corporations primarily through its Public Accounts committee and its Select Committee on Nationalized Industries. Annual reports are examined and debated, and shortcomings and inconsistencies may prove embarrassing to the responsible authorities. Thus, the political ramifications of inefficiency and incompetency serve as a spur to good operational practices. Further, individual members of Parliament may contact governing boards with complaints or advice from their constituents—another way of discovering and remedying ills.

Recent Trends

When the Conservative party was returned to power in 1951, one of the important questions in the minds of the British people was what effect this would have on the future of the planned economy. The mere fact that the Tories were victorious is an interesting commentary on the nature of British socialism—and, perhaps, socialism in general. To many, the concept of socialism with its attacks on a free enterprise system conveys the idea of an all powerful governmental bureaucracy—rigid, intransigent, domineering—which will stifle freedom, political as well as economic. The British experience contrasts sharply with that fear. But more to the point, would the Conservatives, despite their earlier contribution to the rise of the British welfare state, seek to dismantle the economic apparatus which the Laborites had erected since 1945? Would they junk the paraphernalia of restrictions and controls which Labor had imposed? The Conservative answers to these questions were neither so affirmative as the socialistically minded feared nor as the advocates of free enterprise might have hoped. In fact, the history of economic and political developments in Great Britain over the past dozen years throws considerable light on the British politico-economic system broadly and on the differences—ideological and practical —which separate the major British parties.

Throughout the period of Labor dominance the Conservatives in the House of Commons had played their role of "loyal opposition" in typical fashion, questioning, examining, criticizing the bills which the Labor leadership advanced, and the House of Lords, primarily conservative but without much power, was even more antagonistic. Only in one instance, however, was the conflict between the two serious in nature. For the most part the Conservatives were making the normal political noises for partisan purposes in the hope that they would ultimately be returned in a majority by the British electorate. Their objections to the Labor laws were minor; their concerns were with the details of legislation; their objective was constructive criticism with party overtones. On the basic issues and policies the disagreement between Laborites and Conservatives was considerably less than the sound and fury of debate might have led one to believe. And how could it be otherwise? The pragmatic circumstances which prompted Labor's actions were as inescapable for the Tories. The need for centralized direction of the nation's economy to insure the most rapid recovery from the ravages of war was too obvious for the game of partisan politics to be played to the full. Besides, if one overlooked the phrases of Conservative leaders, so replete with the shibboleths of free enterprise, and examined carefully the party's platform of 1945, one could not help being struck with the similarity to that of the Labor party. It hardly behooved the Tories, therefore, to demonstrate too much opposition to a course of action to which they themselves were more or less committed.

Yet with similarity there still remained difference—both of

degree and kind. And with the Conservative victory it began to show itself—slowly but surely. Though there was no abrupt and drastic change, the evidence was there. Probably the most significant change which could be observed was in the area of nationalization, and it was on this score that the two parties had their most genuine difference of opinion in the preceding half-dozen years. Labor had nationalized, among other things, the iron and steel industry, but it had done so with a degree of reluctance and over the serious objections of the Conservative camp. The reason for this was that while the iron and steel industry met at least one of Labor's criteria for nationalization, it did not meet most. Realistically, Labor saw the industry as being of such importance in the economy that it should be nationalized to assure its optimum use as an instrument of national economic planning. But iron and steel was not a "sick" industry; it was not beset with the troubles which plagued others so as to make them ripe for nationalization. In addition, the very importance of the industry had already brought it under close government supervision, so that it was highly unlikely that it could have stood as an obstacle in the road of economic progress.

The Conservatives had argued strenuously against the nationalization, and when they regained political ascendancy they proceeded to denationalize iron and steel as well as long distance road hauling. This, however, was as far as they went; no further denationalization was sought, and the nature of the nationalized industries remained essentially the same as it had been under Labor. The only other "trend" in this matter which the Conservatives established was not to undertake any more nationalizing activities. This action and lack of action illustrates both the similarities and differences of the Labor and Conservative approaches. The Conservatives did not want to turn back the clock nor could they. Yet by temperament and outlook they were considerably more committed to the concept of economic freedom than were the Laborites. They were more cautious than their opponents in the imposition of controls and more anxious to relax such controls whenever the opportunity arose. And on the matter of nationalization, they had to be more fully convinced than their opponents that the need for socializing an industry was so pressing that it could no longer be avoided. At the same time, however, it should be remembered that the Laborites were not fanatical in their rush to substitute public for private ownership or to clamp numerous controls on the economic activity of the nation. Though their socialist orientation led them to take a dim view of the virtues of capitalism, they were fairly cautious in drafting the blueprint of governmental intervention.

As a matter of fact, while a militant segment of the Labor party is still committed to a program of increased nationalization, the party as a whole seems to have had some second thoughts about this line of approach. In the early 1950's the party listed a number of industries which it proposed to investigate as possible fields of nationalization, but it did not advance specific proposals for so doing. By 1957 the Laborites had retreated still farther from the position that nationalization was a *sine qua non* of an equalitarian society. Instead, the party proposed government purchase of shares in private industry as a way of expressing influence in those segments of the economy which would continue to remain in private hands. Thus the chief nationalization goal of the Labor party remains only in the desire to re-nationalize the iron and steel industry and long distance hauling.

The reasons behind the changed Labor attitude are several. In the first place, nationalization did not restore sick industries to a status of robust economic health. It should not have been expected to accomplish this miracle, but for those who may have hoped for too much from this change the failure to achieve greater efficiency and productivity loomed larger than any success in halting further deterioration in the businesses nationalized. Secondly, private business has at times underwritten massive propaganda campaigns against nationalization as the remedy for industrial ills. Thirdly in view of the results achieved, a goodly portion of the Labor party membership began to question this phase of the party's program. These factors combined in developing a public opinion which Labor feared would be translated into antagonistic votes should the nationalizing issue be emphasized too strongly, and as a result, except for a small hard core minority, the party position on public ownership became much more moderate in tone.

The differences between the two major British political parties —and the similarities—on the issue of nationalization has also been apparent in the area of economic planning. While both parties have made a commitment to the necessity for such planning, the extent and the type have varied. The Conservatives have tended to favor less planning than the Laborites, and they have placed a greater reliance on indirect rather than direct controls. Additionally, as circumstances have changed and the economy improved the Tories have been quicker to dismantle these controls and regulatory practices which were in existence. Again a comparison of the two opposing viewpoints indicates a necessary identity of unavoidable direction, but a conceptual distinction which prompts a diversity of procedure. The Labor party can no more avoid its dedication to socialist principles than the Conservative group can avoid its capitalistic heritage. But both parties find empirically a basis for modification of basic principles.

The essence of the subtle yet important distinction in the motivations of the Labor and Conservative parties is perhaps best understood in their respective actions relative to a redistribution of income and the creation of a more egalitarian society. Both are committed to the welfare state principle, but how much of a welfare state remains a point of difference. The Tories are sold on full employment and the provision of a minimum living standard for all, but at the same time they wish to stimulate free enterprise through various incentives which help to maintain a considerable disparity between wealth and moderate comfort. In the same vein, the Conservatives have generally favored some nominal payments by the public for services rendered by the state, support of welfare activities from insurance plans rather than general tax revenues, some sort of means test for the issuance of direct relief, and, in the American fashion, the establishment of private welfare programs to supplant services rendered by the government. Not that the Laborites reject all such ideas; it was they who first initiated charges for national health services. But they did so primarily in the face of economic emergency not as a matter of principle. The Conservatives, more recently, have also utilized indirect taxes—bearing more heavily on lower income groups—to supplement national revenues. In addition, tax benefits to those in the higher income brackets add to the monetary return of the economically privileged. One further development, still in its embryonic stage, signals another point of difference between the two parties. Labor has been proposing a change in the educational system which would revamp the traditional elementary and secondary schools. The British system has had elite overtones and Labor may wish to modify this to some degree.

In summary, today's political picture in Britain presents a peculiar mixture of consensus and difference. Neither party can give vent to its normal ideological leaning nor can either forget its traditions and orientation. The Conservatives still tend to view the programs for the improvement of the masses as a matter of *noblesse oblige* while the Labor group sees such programs as a matter of fundamental human rights. The Tories—albeit somewhat half-heartedly—continue to reflect on the glory of the empire and resent the reduced status of Britain in the international arena. The Laborites seem to take a more pragmatic view on these matters and accept the revision of the empire with better grace; some even lean to disengagement and pacifism. Both parties have readily accepted the challenge of Britain's post-war economic circumstances, but both have modified essential doctrine in the interest of producing electoral success. And—as something of an anomaly—each party has its extreme wing which enunciates a dogma of contrast with its opposite number but which for all practical purposes does not exercise an influential voice in party councils.

As a final commentary on the British scene the voices of the

Britons themselves may prove illuminating. It is the British people who, after all, must live with the systems devised by their leaders and who must react to the particulars of programs as they affect the various aspects of everyday life. With the idea of getting this viewpoint this writer interviewed a number of British citizens in the summer of 1963 seeking to estimate the appraisal of the Briton of the measures which had been enacted since 1945. Two such interviews were especially revealing, but it should be noted that discussions with Britons in various lines of endeavor produced the mixture of opinion which one might expect from a similar series in the United States. It will be seen that the opinions expressed tend to corroborate the foregoing analysis of the party positions and the economic situation.

Walter J. Langford, Headmaster of an English grammar school just outside of London, expressed the opinion that most Britons were committed to the concept of the welfare state but disagreed among themselves as to whether nationalization of private enterprise was the best way to achieve this end. He felt that there was no question that the national health service was working well and that the vast majority of British citizens were happy with the results. He further saw that the lack of revenue occasioned by the physical circumstances confronting Britain after World War II was a principal factor in the manner in which the British economy had evolved. When queried about the potentialities of bureaucratic despotism in the nationalized industries he replied that the public retained adequate control over such industries through their representatives in Parliament and referred to the content of the programs of the British Broadcasting Corporation as an excellent example. One especially noteworthy feature of Mr. Langford's opinion deserves some particular thought. As part of the meaning of the "welfare state" he indicated that it incorporated the idea that those who benefited most from a society should contribute most to the welfare of all members of the society. In other words, the economically well-to-do whose position of wealth is due in large measure to the nature of the society in which they function have a responsibility to assist the economically underprivileged—a responsibility that can be "enforced" by government through tax schedules which fall more heavily on the rich than on the poor.

This concept of the responsibility of wealth is not in the least a novel idea, and in the United States Andrew Carnegie and others outlined in some detail the social burden which wealth entails. Of course, for the American "captains of industry" the emphasis was on the free recognition of such responsibility by the wealthy in their enlightened self-interest, and the doctrine of responsibility was enunciated primarily for the purpose of avoiding governmental coercion in meeting it. For American capitalists, the ideal economy was one in which government was restrained from intervening so that men of inventiveness, ingenuity, and ambition could push ahead and produce goods and services in such number that all the people would ultimately benefit. And from their own conception of largesse these men who amassed fortunes in the process should donate freely to charities and social improvements. Taxes which penalized the rich simply deadened incentive and burdened the economy. But the American "gospel of wealth" takes too little account of two things which may be inferred from the British position as enunciated by Mr. Langford. In the first place, too little emphasis has been placed in American thought on the importance of the total social and economic milieu which permits the entrepreneur to operate and too much on the abilities of the entrepreneur himself. This is not to demean or belittle the man of genius or even business acumen. But it must be recognized that the success of any enterprise must depend to a great degree on the availability and caliber of raw materials, a large number of technicians and laborers, and a consuming public which is willing and able to absorb the production which occurs. In the broader sense, public dissatisfaction with shoddy goods, poor wages, high prices, etc. can create a climate of discontent and social disturbance which can deprive the entrepreneur of his opportunities—no matter how gifted. In brief, the industrialist cannot be separated from his environment. Secondly, the acceptance of that social and economic responsibility which stems from great wealth has not always been ready. And in that circumstance it becomes more understandable that the many would turn to government for assistance when the few indicated a reluctance to share more fully the benefits they had derived from the total society. Even so, the idea of taxing the rich to benefit the poor has not been applied too strenuously in this country.

Professor E. V. Donnison of the London School of Economics commented at greater length on the British situation. To begin with he exhibited the somewhat typical British amusement with the use of the word "socialism" to describe Great Britain's economy and opined that too many Americans had a tendency to infer too much about Britain's status from the loose use of terminology which was not exactly accurate. While conceding that the economy surely displayed characteristics which could be described as socialistic, he explained that the British themselves thought of their system as being one of "managed capitalism." As a matter of fact, he said, British experience with a mixed economy and public understanding of the factors involved had made the use of such a label as socialism practically irrelevant. Even such an item as nationalization—*as an element of socialism* —was not a feature of political discussions. Instead nationalization has its advocates and antagonists not as a tenet of ideology but as a good or bad pragmatic solution to a particular economic problem. This, said Professor Donnison, is the current attitude displayed by the British public. They are much less concerned with ideological debates, with the platitudes of Tories or Laborites, with the "pointing with pride" and "viewing with alarm" of politicians who deal in broad doctrinal analysis, than they are with a down to earth discussion of specific and pressing problems. They want to know what is the proposal of each party with regard to providing adequate housing for all people, not what are the theoretical advantages of public versus private housing developments. They want to know precisely what is planned in the field of educational development, not the hypothetical virtues of private as opposed to public educational systems. In short, their plight has been so intense and their experience so long that the parade of horrors depicted by the opponents of this or that ideology no longer hold much meaning—or much fear. Practical solutions of practical problems are what is demanded, regardless of any appellation attached.

To the extent that socialism does exist in Great Britain, Professor Donnison went on, it does represent a free choice of this arrangement by British leadership and public but in part it was unavoidable. His analysis of this inevitability, however, had a slightly different emphasis than that which has already been given of the impact of war. More to the point, he said, were the poor working conditions in many industries, the labor movement which sought an amelioration of such conditions, and the reluctance or intransigence of industrialists in responding to labor's demands. Inefficiency under private ownership was notorious in some areas, and quasi-mergers and other techniques were used to preserve marginal operators thus contributing still further to the inefficiency of the total industry. In these circumstances the natural result was an insistence on governmental intervention or direct participation in the economy even without the other factors which argued for public direction. This is particularly intriguing in view of the American tendency to describe any economic action by government as socialism. Professor Donnison pointed out that the miners' unions were basically *conservative* in outlook and leadership, but that in seeking specific remedies for the ills of their employment they had to turn to government—not as an expression of any ideological belief but simply as a practical means of getting the job done. Similarly, he continued, nationalization was as much a product of insoluble labor-management disputes of long standing as it was the implementation of socialist dogma.

In commenting on the political ramifications of the competing economic doctrines in England, Professor Donnison made a cogent statement the significance of which is frequently overlooked by the average observer. There is often a temptation on the part of American critics of British society to view the political contest between the Conservatives and Laborites as a battle between capitalism and socialism almost exclusively. Well, we have already noted the fallacy of this assumption in part by outlining the similarity in economic outlook between the two groups. But beyond this it must be remembered that electoral contests in Britain as in the United States involve much more than alternate approaches to the solution of economic problems. A labor victory can no more be attributed solely to the advocacy of nationalization than a Republican victory in America could be attributed solely to the advocacy of a balanced national budget. A political victory by a particular party in either country is always the result of many factors—the issues confronting the country, the personalities and popularity of the party leaders, the economic status of the nation at the time, the stability or instability of the international arena, the mood of the voters, etc. It would be erroneous then to over-generalize, from the results of any one election, the economic development to be expected.

In view of Britain's long experience with socialist movements and the problems which she faced in the post-war world it might seem a bit surprising to some not that Britain has a degree of socialism but that she does not have more. Professor Donnison provided another insight on this score. The Labor party leadership he noted has been traditionally composed of middle class intellectuals. Their commitment to socialism has been rational and humanitarian not militant and fanatical. Altruism rather than dialectical materialism has been the guiding motif. This did not make them any the less socialists, but it tended to modify their fervor with a liberal tradition and to suggest a concrete appraisal of facts before action rather than a blind acceptance of doctrinal dictation. Thus nationalization was not an article of faith; it had to be justified rationally as did other economic measures. The Marxist monolithic state had no appeal for such leaders. In many respects British Labor leadership bore a striking resemblance to that of Norman Thomas' Socialist party leadership in the United States. And for that matter, the followers—the vast body of labor unions who made up a sizeable segment of the Labor party—were not fervent advocates of socialism per se. Their aim has never been the renovation of society according to some grandiose scheme. Rather, they have been interested in the more limited objective of securing an improvement in working conditions and living standards for themselves and for their families. In these circumstances the British development is more clarified and better understood. Moderation has been the keynote, both economically and politically. That this permitted the Tories, by a slight modification of their own position, to compete more effectively for votes seems to have been less important than the conversion of the Conservatives to a viewpoint which incorporates much of the Labor party's platform.

As to the theory and practice of modern British socialism Professor Donnison had a number of pertinent thoughts, some of which should be very disconcerting to socialism's critics. Socialist theory, he admitted, does aim at a certain equalitarianism. But this still leaves two major problems unsettled and debated both between the major parties and within the Labor party itself. First, what is the best way to achieve such equalitarianism? Recognizing that even if one accepts equalitarianism as a virtue, and further that absolute equalitarianism must be an ideal never completely realized, what measures are most likely to approach that ideal without having worse effects than the situation they are designed to improve? No unanimity on this question exists. Second, there is an even more fundamental debate, says Professor Donnison, on the meaning of equalitarianism. Does it mean "equality," or does it mean "equality of opportunity"? The two are obviously quite different and call for different legislative tactics. It is also obviously true that the measures enacted by the British Parliament since 1945 have in different degrees attempted to forward both concepts. While equality of opportunity seems to have received greater attention as the ideal to be gained, equality as such has not been overlooked. Politically, at least in terms of voting, equality has been sought. Economically, equality has meant a minimum living standard for all and has been pursued through direct governmental controls, direct assistance, compulsory insurance schemes, minimum wage laws and other devices. Above that minimum, equality of opportunity permits the more able to rise. At any rate, the debate continues.

Professor Donnison felt that a degree of equalitarianism, however defined, had been achieved in Great Britain but that distribution of income remained highly inconsistent. He noted that tax incentives and fringe benefits to the more affluent portion of the population accounted to a great extent for the continuing income disparity between the relatively poor and the moderately well-to-do. He also said that there might be a tendency to overemphasize tax policies as a tool for income redistribution. While taxes of various sorts do have this aim, he continued, the more immediate objective was to raise governmental revenue for national defense and other purposes.

Several of the most cherished clichés of socialism's antagonists were neatly excised by Professor Donnison's verbal surgery, and his opinions were confirmed at least superficially by this writer's personal observations. That lack of efficiency so frequently charged against public enterprise by the advocates of free enterprise is missing in Great Britain. Really, the degree of efficiency has increased—to the extent possible given the nature of the industry—since the government has replaced private owners. This is not to say that every nationalized enterprise is free from all imperfection, but it is to say that the degree of efficiency in the public corporation compares favorably with that of the private corporation. In this same area, the charge of lack of incentive with the elimination of the profit motive is of dubious validity. Why should the workers lack incentive? Their wages are better and their conditions of labor improved. The managerial cadre wishes to improve itself for personal reasons which would apply in the world of private business, and, of course, there is the more subtle motive of the political repercussions which might ensue from the poor performance of "bureaucrats." And then there is the matter of freedom in a "regimented" society. Laws are, by and large, restraints on individuals and groups, and the larger the number of laws and regulations the greater the limitation on human freedom. But an accurate appraisal of the verity of this dictum requires a more empiric observation. Anyone who sees Great Britain at first hand can have no question as to the high degree of British political freedom and the great respect accorded civil rights. Public discussions abound on any subject, and the prophet of the unorthodox may freely put his ideas before his peers in the arena of general debate. This tradition of open discussion which has so long been the pride of British democracy remains unimpaired. The very fact that Labor was voted out of office is a significant commentary on the extent of political freedom which exists. Economically, of course, the vast array of government enterprises, regulations, controls, taxes, etc., do impose minimal shackles on the freedom of the individual entrepreneur to run his business as he sees fit. The whole concept of economic planning necessitates restriction on free choice in the economic realm. To that extent freedom in the broadest sense is curtailed. But businessmen still maintain a significant degree of choice among alternatives. Farmers are free to conduct their operations as they choose so long as they maintain a minimum efficiency. Trade unions remain virile and demanding. And can it be said that economic freedom is cramped when the end results of the imposition of controls are greater employment, higher wages, greater leisure, the modification of economic distress for the aged and infirm, and a general improvement in the nation's economic position?

As regards the future of Great Britain's economy, one thing remains clear, Professor Donnison concluded. The planned economy will continue. As was outlined before, both the Labor and Conservative parties remain firmly wedded to the conviction that England's circumstances require a continuation of national planning. What exact form this planning will take in the future remains to be seen. Further nationalization on any large scale is unlikely. The relaxation of existing controls must depend on internal and external developments and the predominance of Tories or Laborites in the national legislature. The introduction of innovations in the planning pattern will depend on the inventiveness of the planners and the attractiveness of the plans to the general public. But so long as England's economic condition remains precarious and the international environment continues highly competitive and/or threatening we can expect to see a prolongation of Britain's managed capitalism.

STUDY QUESTIONS AND PROJECT SUGGESTIONS

1. Was it practically inevitable that Great Britain would develop a more socialist economy after World War II?

2. What are the basic features of "Keynesian" economics?

3. What guidelines were set by the Labor party to determine if a particular industry should be nationalized?

4. Compare the essential provisions of Britain's "socialized medicine" plan and America's "medicare."

5. To what extent do the Laborites and Tories differ in their positions on the welfare state?

6. Evaluate the proposition that the wealthy have a special responsibility to contribute to the welfare of all the members of society.

7. Has British socialism led to a curtailment of political and economic freedom?

CHAPTER 11

CONTEMPORARY FRENCH SOCIALISM

Like Great Britain, France has long been exposed to the doctrines of various socialist groups. It too has had a long life as a national entity, and to a far greater extent has suffered the devastation of recurring international hostilities. Unlike Great Britain, however, the French population is considerably more heterogeneous, and this has produced a spectrum of political parties running from the extreme left to the extreme right philosophically. It has also resulted in a leadership which has been regularly uncertain because it depended on a coalition support which was not always forthcoming. All of these factors have, of course, had a bearing on the course of the French economy.

France's long history as a sovereign state has led to a variety of political structures ranging from complete autocracy to the most exaggerated "democracy," and each adventure in politics had a concomitant economic result. After its emergence from feudalism France's economic organization became one of essentioally free enterprise, but a free enterprise operation in which the respective segments of society had even less faith in each other than was the case in either Great Britain or the United States. Thus the stage was set for the government to enter the economic arena as referee of the conflicting economic interests.

Today, even within a major sector of the economy there is the same division which seems to characterize the society as a whole. In agriculture, for example, there are tenants, sharecroppers, ordinary laborers, and peasant proprietors each with a slightly different interest, and within the land-owning groups the proprietors of large estates may hold different viewpoints than those who have small plots. The dedication of the French farmer to the land is an important facet of national beliefs, and the desire of each to own land—no matter how small an acreage —has had a bearing on political moves. At the same time, this dedication to one's own land has made the French agriculturist extremely individualistic and independent minded which outlook does not always accord with those political philosophies committed to redistribution of land through state edict. It is a rather interesting phenomenon in French life that the nonlanded, subsequent to World War I, sought governmental assistance in acquiring that land which was so fervently sought, but once having acquired it exhibited a typically individualistic and anti-state attitude which left them more or less political independents and strongly opposed to the acceptance of such responsibilities of loyal citizens as paying taxes.

French farmers, like those in the United States, turned to organization as another way of securing their demands, and such unions were generally socialistically oriented. Later, they actually formed political parties of their own which, contrary to what might have been expected, were distinctly conservative in philosophy. The farmers' unions today still retain a socialist connection, and many farmers vote for Communist party candidates, but as a whole the individual farmer remains individualistic and conservative though expressing himself politically in votes for radical candidates as a protest. He is interested, of course, in government sponsored measures such as subsidies and protective tariffs on agricultural imports, but beyond this his socialism or radicalism is more nominal than real.

The situation in industry is not dissimilar. The tradition of French industrial production has been the relatively small business in which craftsmanship and pride of workmanship predominated. The press of the industrial revolution and the demands of national defense wrought a significant change in organization for production and produced a split in opinion between the large and the small entrepreneur. The growth of giant industry has made socialism more acceptable to a large segment of the workers who see little difference between big business and big government as owner and operator of enterprise. Simultaneously, there was in France a movement which both supported and opposed the main thread of socialist development. Trade unionism developed in France along syndicalist lines. To the extent that the movement sought to improve the lot of the industrial proletariat it fell within the objectives of the broader socialist development. But to the extent that the syndicalists sought a reorganization of industry in which the workers would evolve fairly autonomous economic and political control at the local level, the cause of centralized, state directed socialism was not well served. By the time of the post World War II era the French trade union movement had divided into three different camps. The largest and most influential of the groups was the *Confédération Générale du Travail,* communist dominated and numbering about 1.5 million members. A second, of more democratic persuasion, is the *Force Ouvrière* which controls approximately 500,000 members. And the third major body is the *Confédération Française des Travailleurs Chrétiens,* the Catholic union which may or may not share the aspirations of one or the other trade unions. Thus, while the three unions superficially may share common aims, political or other manifestations of their activities may make them competitors rather than allies in a common cause.

In business too one finds in France the same division evident in the other branches of the economy and discovers also part of the explanation for the rise of socialism to the degree to which it exists presently. As in the case of the farmers, the little businessman in France strives to be his own man. The small shopkeeper, the individual artisan, the self-owned business—these are the ideals of French commerce. The businessman yearns for freedom and independence of action rather than material affluence, and as such, he is not an ardent socialist of any stripe. Big business, on the other hand, does strive for the amassing of fortunes, and in this pursuit it has attempted strenuously to shape the course of government policy over the years. Big business shares with little business a desire to interdict governmental restraint in commerce, but more, it seeks active governmental action in support of its own objectives, perhaps to the discomfiture of the small entrepreneur. Through control of the Bank of France, influence in the national legislature, development of public opinion by its newspapers, and the force of its associations, big business had things pretty much its own way in the late nineteenth and early twentieth centuries. It was conservative and autocratic and demonstrated too little concern for the welfare of the thousands of workers employed in its various enterprises. By nature, and because of its desire for survival, a significant segment of the big business community collaborated with the Nazis or the Vichy regime following the fall of France during World War II. With the liberation this sympathy with the enemy was not quickly forgotten. In a number of cases the property of collaborators was confiscated. In other instances private business was nationalized. Such was the fate of the Bank of France, the Renault automobile establishment, the coal mines, gas and electricity, and the insurance business. But the big business community was not thoroughly squashed. Individually and collectively the large entrepreneurs have regained their influence and their property. The failure of the Fourth Republic was due in part to the lack of support which they gave, and the advent of the Fifth Republic and the ascendancy of General Charles De Gaulle is due in large measure to the decision by big business that he was the most attractive of the potential leaders. This position—past and present—of the French capitalists is both a stimulant to socialism and a deterrent. Its failure to consider the French worker more than it did sped the acceptance of socialist philosophy. Its adamant stand and its governmental influence serve as a constant obstacle to the expansion of socialist practice.

The French population, in short, is highly fragmented. It is traditionally individualistic with the possible exception of the industrial proletariat. It is made up of those who have been unalterably committed to the maintenance of the status quo, those who have been invariably motivated to the improvement of the lot of the masses, those whose basic allegiance is to the Roman Catholic church, those who see Marx' dialectical materialism as the only realistic approach to human relationships, those who are monarchists, those who are democrats, and those whose political, social, and economic philosophies boil down to a momentary appraisal of their own best interests. Out of this mixture and burdened with the aftermath of war and depression the French leadership has had to devise policies which would carry France forward in the contemporary world. After World War II these policies have tended more and more in the direction of national economic planning, but they have not shunted aside the long tradition of economic individualism. Probably the most striking post-war development is not the extent of socialistic influence, but the fact that France, despite its disunity, has made a more startling economic recovery than any European belligerent except Germany.

The Socialist Party

Although a number of the French political parties have a collectivist outlook, notably the Communists, it is the Socialist party which is the prime exponent of the economic doctrines of orthodox socialism. Of course, practically all the political groupings including De Gaulle's *Union pour la Nouvelle République*

(UNR) accept a certain amount of social reform as necessary and desirable, and the Radical Socialists and the *Mouvement Républicain Populaire* were at one time distinctly socialist in orientation. But these last two have become moderate center parties leaving the Communists and the Socialists to expound the doctrines of the left.

The Socialists' history has been replete with prominent leaders, and its political fortunes—as is true of most parties—have been affected by events and attitudes having little relation to economic doctrine. In the Dreyfus affair at the turn of the century, for example, Jules Guesde, the Marxist, saw the whole affair as a trumped up struggle and advised ignoring the matter. Jean Jaurès, on the other hand, saw the matter as a vital conflict in which the military leadership, the aristocracy, and the clergy were attempting to maintain their positions of power by making Dreyfus a scapegoat for the graft and corruption which were rampant. Later, Jaurès, influenced by a natural humanitarianism inherent in the French socialist movement and by the Marxian dictum of imperialist war, attempted to lead his followers to pacifism and the avoidance of the imminent conflict of World War I. As in the United States this effort was doomed to failure as patriotism submerged pacifism, and Jaurès was assassinated just as the war began. This attitude on the part of the leadership had some adverse effect on the future of the party. Subsequently, after the French defeat in World War II, the fact that some Socialist party leaders cooperated with the Vichy regime hurt the group still more and overshadowed the fact that others had been active members of the resistance movement.

The French socialists—after the mid-nineteenth century—were a curious mixture of the more moderate viewpoint expressed in the earlier socialist developments and the more extreme viewpoint which Marxist doctrine had fostered. Even the "moderates," however, had a history of activism and militancy in the pursuit of their objectives. For a time the communists and socialists were closely related in seeking the aims of the working class, but after the Russian revolution the two broke completely over the refusal of the socialists to accept the Soviet dictated terms for a remodeling of the party machinery to conform to communist standards as a basis for incorporation in the Third International. (The party is still officially known as the *Section Française de l'Internationale Ouvrière* or SFIO for short.) The split left the socialists with a far greater following than the communists, and they gained increasing prominence as a party until, in 1936, under Léon Blum they formed a Popular Front government against fascism with the Radicals and Communists. The leadership was never totally unified, however, and in the aftermath of the Second World War their influence declined.

Following the conclusion of hostilities the Socialist party proclaimed anew the principles and purposes to which it was dedicated. This declaration of 1946 began with the usual statement of intended liberation of the oppressed and the creation of an atmosphere which would permit the free exercise of rights and natural faculties. This was quickly followed by a condemnation of the rule of capitalistic property which had produced antagonistic classes and which permitted the few to live in luxury without labor and the many to labor without enjoying the full fruits of their endeavors. The proclamation went on to note the commonality of the working classes regardless of "philosophical or religious belief" and the intention of the Socialist party to unify the masses in the struggle for their just rights. Then the statement expounded that unique characteristic of French socialism—a partially Marxian heritage combined with typically socialistic moderation:

The Socialist Party is an essentially *revolutionary* party: its goal is to accomplish the substitution for the rule of capitalistic property of a regime in which natural riches and the means of production and exchange will become the property of the community and in which, consequently, classes will be abolished. This transformation, accomplished in the interest of all mankind, can only result from the action of the workers themselves. *Whatever the means* by which it will be carried out, it will thereby constitute the *social revolution!* [1]

Having implied their militancy, the Socialists then went on to emphasize the democratic nature of the party and the importance of democratic processes in achieving socialist goals. A similar dichotomy concluded the statement of principles when the party described itself as being "at once national and international." It wished to retain its independent status, but it did not wish to dissociate itself from the worldwide socialist movement.

A 1958 action program emphasized some of the earlier principles but also indicated a difference in tone from the previous pronouncement. It reiterated the aims of abolishing class barriers and suppressing social injustices, and it paid tribute to the party's former militants—"the most famous as well as the most obscure." But it clarified its gradualistic and moderate stance. Socialism is described as a "doctrine and a moral principle"; its democratic organization is stressed. The Socialist party has always defended republican institutions, stated the program, "because democracy represents an indispensable prerequisite for progress toward Socialism." The party also called attention to its willingness to cooperate or participate in coalition governments, as it had in the past, with those who did not share doctrinal beliefs so long as the welfare of the nation and concepts of social justice were at stake. And as regards the relation between French Socialists and the Soviet Union, the program was outspoken in its assertion of independence and its condemnation of communist practices. Socialists would not, it declared, "make use either of hate or of untruth or of crime in order to establish a new society"; they would not soil the new order with "despair, tortures or blood." The Soviet electorate was characterized as being "deceived by a debauch of hateful, negative propaganda."

Thus it can be seen that the Socialist party today is the legitimate heir in the family of French socialism. It attacks

[1] Steven Muller, ed., *Documents on European Government* (New York: Macmillan, 1963), pp. 129-130. (Italics added.)

capitalism, but proposes a "social" revolution to overthrow it. It is militant in spirit, but moderate in action. It accepts class antagonism, but not class warfare. It uses parliamentary tools to try to build a new society. It is concerned with morality. But despite whatever virtues the party might possess, and despite its earlier popular support, after World War II the influence of the party began to wane. Several contributory factors are discernible.

In the first place, the memory of the Vichy collaborationists could not be completely eliminated from the public mind. The Gallic nature was not quick to forgive these transgressions. As a corollory to this, the Communists, with their greater fidelity to Soviet leadership, had been extremely active and prominent within the resistance movement, and their stock rose proportionately. By virtue of their newly enhanced popularity the Communists were able to rise to positions of leadership in the largest of the national trade unions, the C.G.T., and their aggressive attitude seemed, at least momentarily, to appeal to the workers. Thus in 1947, when the Socialists objected to the tactics employed, the C.G.T. split, with the larger segment of members remaining with the Communist leadership, and with the Socialists losing further ground in popular appeal.

Perhaps more important was the failure of the Socialist party to adjust to the new political and economic environment in postwar France. It had been bothered earlier by the divisive tendencies of militancy and moderation; its contemporary status and appeal remained similarly clouded. In the new environment the industrial proletariat was undergoing a change in character. It was diversified rather than unified; it was mildly antagonistic internally; and it was losing some of its aggressive tendencies as it improved its economic lot. The Socialists responded in part to the new context by modifying its beliefs in public ownership, seeking rather to revamp French capitalism in the interest of more equitable distribution of income for the whole society instead of just the "workers." But the leaders insisted on clinging to the old doctrines and the old slogans which implied a revolutionary credo—though they were certainly not revolutionary activists, and on preserving a high degree of autonomy in the party hierarchy—especially in their parliamentary grouping—while they were preaching democracy. An attempt to make the party consistent in practice and principle by transforming it into a British-type labor party was defeated by the leadership. The results might have been foretold. For those who were actual militants, phrases and catch-words were not enough. They craved more overt action and went over to the Communists. For those who read the slogans for what they were and found themselves more in accord with what the Socialists actually were doing, gradually and democratically, the constant reference to the revolutionary theme was unsettling, and the tightly-knit leadership remained inconsistent with the greater democracy which such supporters desired. Therefore, even where the Socialists picked up support from the moderates—intellectuals, teachers, civil servants, and conservative workers—to replace that lost from the hard core proletariat, it was less than enthusiastic.

Two other causes have contributed further to the decline of Socialist party strength and influence. For one thing it seems to have alienated the youth of the country. The inconsistency between public image and party practice led to a decline in membership, and the young, naturally inclined to greater activity and less theorizing, have turned their interests in other directions. But more than this, the party's rules discriminate against the younger members by requiring five years membership before the opportunity to perform any significant party function occurs. Only those who meet such requirement may edit a party paper, be a delegate to the party congress, become a member of the executive committee, or stand for Parliament. The Socialists may be dying of old age.

The other problem which has caused the Socialists trouble is again a conflict between theory and practice. It involved the question of colonialism. True to the socialist creed the French Socialists have generally espoused the cause of anti-imperialism and the reduction of military expenditures. But in post-war France the Socialists again found themselves in an anomalous position. If they remained out of coalition governments they ran the risk of an exaggerated influence being exercised by the extreme left or the extreme right, but if they cooperated in "center" coalitions they had to compromise certain principles. Deciding on the path of cooperation they found themselves supporting a war in Indo-China and policies designed to retain Tunisia, Morocco, and Algeria as parts of the French empire. It was an intolerable, though perhaps inescapable, dilemma, and despite the pragmatic virtue of the position the Socialists once more lost a certain amount of support from liberal elements.

In spite of this waning influence and support, the Socialists have managed to remain second or third in numbers of votes polled in the national elections following World War II, and they have participated in several coalition governments. When they have been outside of the "government" they have played the role of "constructive opposition." With the De Gaulle leadership they have tended to support foreign policy decisions, but they have objected to financial aid to Catholic schools and to various domestic policies the cost of which they believed would weigh too heavily on the working classes.

Another Mixed Economy

Out of the social, political, and economic heterogeneity of French history there has arisen, as might be expected, a mixed economic organization of the type previously examined in the United States and Great Britain, with a slightly greater degree of state ownership. Tracing the development of the mixed economy does not illustrate a consistent pattern of evolution. The network of controls, rules, and state enterprise has resulted from the ideas and actions taken sporadically by ministers and premiers whose political stripes have ranged from conservative to Marxist. This, combined with the fractured interests of the population, makes it difficult to discern any central theme which has been primarily responsible for the areas of governmental intervention or the process of regulation. State activity is observable in many sectors of the economy, but some of them are of such minor significance that they seem questionable as appropriate targets of control, while other more important aspects remain relatively untouched. Similarly the pattern of social services looks more like a hodge-podge of responses to specific demands rather than the implementations of a carefully considered philosophy of societal upgrading.

The instability of French politics has been in large measure a contributing factor to this patchwork economic mosaic. Coalition governments have long been prey to two marauders. On the one hand they have had to be too receptive to the demands of competing interest groups in order to retain the popular support necessary to a working majority in the Parliament. On the other any sweeping program initiated by such a coalition could founder quickly with the unseating of the ruling group by a dissatisfied legislature. Thus there was a sort of "stop and go" nature to economic development which gave to France a very uneven progress. And, perhaps overriding all other political questions, there has been the constant concern with the agricultural segment of the society. Given the emphasis on agriculture in France this is not a surprising political concern, but this emphasis has had significant ramifications. The continuing love for the soil and the desire for ownership, as well as the generally individualistic nature of the French farmer has tended to perpetuate the marginal operator and to deter the acceptance of the large farm and modern farming methods. Moreover, there has been a tendency to exaggerate the importance of the farm vote and to fail to take account of the problems of distribution of agricultural products the rising cost of which has made French food prices among the highest on the continent.

Economic Planning

Economic planning is not an innovation in France though its full impact is a contemporary phenomenon. As far back as the 18th century royal interference succeeded "Colbertism" which brought porcelain and tapestry production under state control. For the typical Frenchman this was *dirigisme* or *étatisme* which was contrary to prevailing concepts of laissez-faire, but it was a precedent which, two centuries later, pointed the way to the modern mixed economy. Planning as a broad program of governmental surveillance of the total economy is, however, a product of the second quarter of the twentieth century.

Modern economic plans since the 1930's have been essentially of two types.[2] The first kind of plan has been a broad program of socio-politico-economic reform seeking to encompass the totality of public life. The second type has been essentially economic in nature with only minor political connotations. In the former category, the Popular Front Program of 1936 is exemplary. It was not as neatly and comprehensively drawn as it might have been, but it aimed at and succeeded in achieving nationalization of the Bank of France and the armament industries, imposition of a graduated income tax, governmental control of production of wheat together with a guarantee of minimum prices for this grain, and a program of collective bargaining and compulsory arbitration of labor disputes. Whatever shortcomings were apparent in this approach to curing economic ills it was a major step in the direction of economic planning, but its prospective efficacy was never fully realized because of the advent of World War II.

The second sweeping plan was a product of wartime experiences and theorizing about the country's future when peace

[2] See E. Drexel Godfrey, Jr., *The Government of France* (New York: Crowell, 1961), pp. 88-91.

came again. The National Council of the Resistance, with support from practically all elements of French politics, produced, in 1944, a charter calling for some radical socio-economic changes. The charter sought nationalization of industry in the energy and resources fields, greater control of the banking and insurance businesses, anti-trust legislation, and a greater voice for labor in industrial management. When a provisional government was established after the war the nationalization schemes were rapidly enacted, but the other proposals were only partially adopted.

Subsequently, planning in France became primarily economic with only incidental political overtones. This was the result essentially of the thinking of Jean Monnet translated into action by the recommendations of the Commissariat General of the Plan of Modernization and Equipment (*Commissariat Général au Plan*) to the National Assembly. The Commissariat had been established shortly after the conclusion of hostilities at the direction of Monnet. The first plan, covering a five year period, was dedicated not only to the general reconstruction of the war-torn economy but to special action in eight basic sectors of that economy: electricity, cement, steel, coal, transportation, fuel, fertilizers, and farm machinery. Investment, both public and private, was channeled into these areas to develop national production and foreign trade and to up the general standard of living. With the help of funds coming from the United States under the European Recovery Program, the objectives of this plan—covering the period from 1947 to 1952—were generally attained. The second so-called Hirsch plan sought to increase national income by 25% over a four year period by increasing agricultural production, expanding industry and stepping up construction, especially in housing. The emphasis in this period was not only on modernization but on research, cost reduction, and reorganization of distribution methods—particularly of agricultural products—so as to lower consumer prices. Again the record of achievement was impressive. In the third post-war plan the emphasis was again on increased production, but the aims began to have a greater social and political coloration, and, despite the centralization of authority under the Fifth Republic, it was subjected to greater criticism than had been the case previously.

It must be noted that the success of post-war planning in France was not a function purely of the extent of government ownership and operation of productive enterprise. To be sure, this factor did simplify some of the actions taken. But the main principles governing the march to recovery seem to have been cooperation between government and private industry and a resort to indirect methods of control, specifically the government's investment policy. Private investment was induced into specific areas, and, where this proved to be inadequate, government subsidies and loans took up the slack. Though the Commissariat is the principal planning agency for advising the Premier on economic goals and methods, it relies heavily on the advice and suggestions of professional and occupational groups. Advisory commissions of all sorts provide the expertise and experience of the business community upon which government planners may draw.

Government and Business

France has had traditionally a free enterprise economic organization, but, nevertheless, the relations between government and business have been close. The long-time relations gave business the upper hand as it demanded and received from government supports and subsidies of various kinds. This is not surprising as the nature of French politics was such that political support had to be purchased through catering to the wishes of diverse interest groups. But governmental relationship to the economy has not been confined to the satisfaction of the business community. Rather, as has been true in the United States and Great Britain, the French government has been an active participant in economic activity for many years.

Beginning with the establishment of a government monopoly in the manufacture of tobacco products in 1678, the succeeding French administrations expanded the pattern of governmental intervention in and ownership of productive and distributive facilities. Today the government owns and operates the railroads, civil aviation, telephone and telegraphic enterprise, radio and television, the postal service, and match production. Roads, bridges, canals, and ports have been built, and many actions have been taken relative to agriculture and conservation. Hydroelectric facilities have been developed and expanded and improved, housing has been a prime governmental concern. Of course, the manner of government's participation in the economy has not been limited to nationalization of private business.

Among the other techniques of regulation are public investment and direction of private investment into approved channels, price controls, and taxation policies. Taxes are of various sorts, and many are discriminatory only incidentally. In addition to corporate income taxes, there are taxes on practically every stage of a productive process and taxes on most stages of transfer of products. Unquestionably the main intent of such imposts is revenue raising, but they are bound to have certain regulatory effects. Beyond this, subsidies, eclectic export and import licensing, and preferential treatment for selected business endeavors permit the government to exercise a considerable influence on the economy. Much of what the government does is by administrative action, but the more significant moves are either taken directly by the legislature or clearly authorized so as to screen responsible ministers from undue criticism. But the core of the government's ability to direct the economy rests in its capacity to manipulate the nationalized industries and services—the Bank of France, coal, transportation, armaments, and the automobile industry—so that the remainder of economic enterprise must of necessity feel the repercussions.

The "nationalized" industries take two principal forms. On the one hand there are the mixed corporations or national companies. These are enterprises, such as the railroads, in which the government in one way or another came to hold a majority of the stock, but in which private capital is liberally present. This, of course, permits the government to direct the decisions of the controlling board. The other, and more normal, nationalized industry is operated as a public corporation—such as the T.V.A. in the United States—with almost exclusively government capital. They exist as separate legal entities, though as in Great Britain, there is over-all supervision from some designated ministry. Each industry is managed by a board of directors on which there is representation from labor, management, and the consuming clientele of the industry. However, unlike the situation in Great Britain, the managing director of the enterprise is not appointed by the board but by the government. And the increased authority of this individual has naturally enhanced the role of the government in directing the industry.

Another aspect of the operation which emphasizes the government's role is that the boards are not authorized to fix prices for the services the industry provides. This is the prerogative of one or another governmental supervising agency. The French boards are unpaid, and, as a result, there tends to be a rather high degree of absenteeism from their deliberations, a fact which further strengthens the position of the general manager. Where the boards do exercise influence it is primarily through the representatives of labor who themselves are under the influence of the communist dominated C.G.T. Needless to say, as in Britain, the legislature keeps a wary eye on the operations of the nationalized industries—especially their financial transactions— through the reports submitted by them and the appraisals of their activities made by the responsible ministers.

Government and Agriculture

The French government's potential for dealing with the agricultural situation is complicated almost to the point of impotency by the fact that the problems of agriculture stem as much from psychological and sociological sources as from technical and economic reasons, and any proposal for reform must face the formidable obstacles of deeply ingrained tradition and the political repercussions of an assault on this emotional fortress. The nature of this tradition emphasizes the very things which need correction—small, marginally viable farms; outmoded farming techniques; production of non-profitable crops; splitting of farm acreage into even smaller parcels through the operation of inheritance laws; continued subsidization of crops which are uneconomical; undue emphasis on the farmer as a political force; catering to the demands of a farm lobby whose bark far surpasses its bite; and reconstruction of the distributive apparatus for farm products which is such an important phase of the agricultural problem from the point of view of the French consumer. Unless one is thoroughly aware of the irrational nature of this problem, the activities of the government undertaken to improve the agricultural situation seem timid and innocuous.

Nevertheless, succeeding French administrations have made some efforts to deal with the farm problem. Price subsidization has been, of course, a prime consideration, but marketing regulations and even land ownership have received some consideration. During the first post-war plan, considerable attention was given to modernization of farming techniques, the introduction of contemporary farm machinery, and improvement in fertilizers. There was, additionally, the introduction of rural extension services under governmental auspices, but the individualistic French farmer did not take readily to the idea of a central government representative giving advice to a dedicated and traditional farmer. Unfortunately, the few short strides made in the direction of modifying the age-old agricultural process were undercut by the continued subsidizing of uneconomic crops and the special privileges granted the producers of specific regions. Despite the extreme prestige and power of the De Gaulle regime under the Fifth Republic, the agricultural sector of the society continues to occupy a somewhat sacrosanct position.

Probably the most significant attempt to revamp the pattern of agricultural production and distribution relates to the latter —though its effects may remain to be felt in the future. The De Gaulle administration has tried to eliminate or modify the use of the Paris central market, *les Halles*, whose sprawling facilities ringed by all night cafés are such a mecca for tourists. Through the years *les Halles* has been the receiving point for all sorts of agricultural products coming from the outlying districts. Here, after handling by various processors and sellers and being subject to a significant amount of spoilage, the products are then shipped to retailers and ultimately to the consumers. Like so many other things in France this practice had become traditional, and the fact that the process added immeasurably to distribution costs —some products, for example, ending up back in the regions from which they came—did little to change the practice. Efforts to establish regional markets have borne some fruit, but *les Halles* continues to hold its position of prominence and to keep the costs of agricultural products to the consumer much higher than they should be if efficiency were improved.

It would be too arrogant to assess the French farm problem in purely economic terms. The small family farm is inefficient. The political pressures of the farm bloc are disproportionate. Subsidies to marginal operators preserve inefficiency. A firm hand could minimize the production of uneconomic crops. The distributive apparatus is clumsy and contributes to unnecessarily high costs. But can one measure effectively the contribution to the national fibre of the land conscious, individualistic, industrious small farmer? Should a degree of inefficiency be tolerated or encouraged in an area whose psychic values may outweigh economic costs? Does the nature of the farming class require its perpetuation relatively unchanged? So long as these questions permit uncertain answers it may be better that French agriculture remain outside the strong mold of directed planning.

Labor and Social Security

The advances made by labor in terms of wages, hours, and conditions of employment in the advanced industrialized countries like Great Britain and the United States have been due largely to the ability of the laboring force to organize and thus exert economic as well as political pressure. In France, the general nature of the French populace combined with the particular history of the labor movement have made such efforts at organization and collective bargaining far less effective than they have been elsewhere. This does not mean that progress has not been made, but it has been more uneven in its development and later in arriving.

Various factors can be delineated as contributing to the state of affairs, not the least of which was the official—if not totally effective—outlawing of trade unions in France until the last quarter of the 19th century. Even where trade unionism existed it was motivated much more by the spirit of syndicalism than it was by that of Christian socialism. This meant that violence, industrial sabotage, and the general strike were accepted as the techniques which would topple the capitalist society, and the more moderate aims of gradual reform and the improvement bit by bit of the living standards of the working masses were more or less shunted aside. Thus, while the Socialists—in the early part of the twentieth century—attempted to secure gradual advances they were deprived of the assistance of the militants in the trade union movement who wanted a total revolution or nothing, and who saw in these piecemeal efforts merely a prolongation of the depressed state of the workers. However, the majority of the working class were not converted to revolutionary syndicalism, and the syndicalists themselves became disillusioned about the possibilities of achieving the goals which they had set. In this atmosphere progress was slow and the stage was set for the later fractionalization of the trade union movement. For a while in the mid-1930's there was a merging of various trade union groupings, but following World War II there developed the split in labor's ranks which has been described previously. That the C.G.T.—the largest of the unions—is communist dominated continues to present a political problem as well as an economic one.

Labor's plight is further heightened in that in each plant or industry there may be represented two or more of the major labor unions, and collective bargaining is secondary to strikes, protests, or jurisdictional disputes. Nevertheless, since 1936 there has been national legislation outlining the scope and method of collective bargaining in industry. The bargaining itself is less than the best in that, especially in view of the opposition expressed by the entrepreneurs, there is no industry-wide bargaining. Agreements are arrived at for different branches of the same industry, or regional agreements are reached which have little relation to each other. The labor negotiators are frequently only moderately competent, and the circumstances under which the government may intervene are severely limited. This does not mean that such negotiations are useless from labor's viewpoint, but it does give the management side a distinct advantage. Again the individualistic nature of the typical Frenchmen seems to work to his disadvantage if he belongs to the working class.

The government does play a more active role in labor relations in the nationalized industries. In those industries which are monopolies such as the coal mines and the gas and electric services collective bargaining is proscribed by law. But, strangely enough, it is in these areas that the government is impelled to grant the most favorable wages, hours, and conditions of employment. It must set standards which clearly indicate its concern for the welfare of the workers. It must not permit the establishment of criteria which private industry could use as a lever to justify a lowering of the living standards of their employees. Thus while the worker is denied a voice in determining his financial return, he is protected by the inherent necessity of the government to forward his interests. In those economic enterprises in which the government position is not monopolistic, insurance, for example, collective bargaining is used. Wage agreements reached must be approved by the responsible minister, but again the tendency is to be liberal in such matters.

As for social security, trade unions had for many years a vision of a comprehensive scheme which would cover all the exigencies of life from unemployment to death. The implementation of this scheme as a whole was never accomplished, but by degrees various laws have been enacted which provide today a wide spectrum of social services comparable to those in Great Britain. While labor and socialist pressures have been primarily responsible for such legislation, other reasons have also been present. The family benefits, for instance, stemmed from conservative sources not so much as an income supplement but as a spur to increased population which had seriously declined in the inter-war period. Other benefits have originated as distinct income supplements provided by the government in the face of low wage rates retained by recalcitrant employers who refused to bow to the suggestions of governments which were so weak that private entrepreneurs could collectively and even individually defy them.

The social services cover a wide range of activities including medical care, accident insurance, unemployment compensation, matrimonial benefits, and death benefits. As a whole the programs are supervised by the Ministry of Labor, but practically they are administered in a highly decentralized manner. Both functional and regional subdivisions exist, and elected boards representing employees and employers help to direct the implementation of the programs in local districts. Since the employees generally outnumber the employer representatives on these boards three to one, the C.G.T. has been able to exercise a significant influence in the development of the programs. Theoretically, the whole program of social services is supposed to be self-financed. Employers and employees share the burden of contributions from which the benefits ultimately flow, with the employers making the greater contribution. As a matter of fact, however, given the nature of the population with its larger number of aged and extremely young, the government has had to make occasional contributions to the insurance funds from other revenues.

SUMMARY

The contemporary French society and its economic structure are that typical combination of conservation and radicalism, free enterprise and paternalism, tradition and innovation, freedom and security which are the hallmarks of the modern complex industrialized nation. As is true of any nation which one may choose, the precise structure of the society reflects vividly the peculiar national traits and history of its people. That which appears to be anomalous becomes clearer when there is some understanding of the deep cleavages which have rent the French people. Few nations have experienced the variety of political, social, and economic movements which have buffeted the French mind. Few peoples seem to have the temperament which gives such conviction to the French convert to a cause. And the position of the Roman Catholic church in French history is probably more significant than in any country except Italy. Against this background, an appreciation of the mixed status of the French economy is clarified. This writer had the opportunity to consult with a number of Frenchmen regarding their impressions of the "socialist" nature of their economy, and again the discussions were revealing. One such interview was especially insightful.

M. François Terré of the Ministry of Justice was particularly helpful in appraising the French system from the French viewpoint. It is always somewhat difficult for a foreign observer to see below the surface of the apparent and to sense the native feelings about economics and politics, so the honest opinions and beliefs of the citizens of any society are invaluable in sub-stantiating or correcting presuppositions and tentative conclu-sions. Once again the superficial observations which can be made about the French system are corroborated by the comments of M. Terré.

The French, of course, are very used to living with "socialism" as a concept and as the program of one or more political parties. They, like the British, have moved beyond a concern with the ideological aspects of socialism which intrigue so many Ameri-cans. They are aware that socialism is neither as good as its proponents have argued nor as bad as its opponents feared. Having experienced socialist political leadership and witnessed socialism as a part of the country's economic organization the French are able to concentrate much more readily on the prag-matic problems of their society without becoming enmeshed in doctrinal clichés of support or antagonism. At the same time, they can and do consistently reexamine politico-economic dogma from whatever source. And it is in this sense that the remarks of a native have special value for the researcher.

In a general vein, M. Terré noted the truism that socialism—considered simply as government owned and operated enter-prise—has the distinct advantage of providing *services* to the population which private enterprise could not provide at a profit. The accuracy of this observation is obvious if one con-siders—in American terms—the cost of delivering the mail if profit and the utmost in efficiency were the criteria of judgment rather than service to the people. He also made the point which contradicts the viewpoint held by many critics of socialism that there has been no apparent loss of initiative or incentive on the part of the French workers in the nationalized industries. Again it may be assumed that from the viewpoint of the worker a "distant" employer whether it be a private entrepreneur or a national government adds or detracts little from the paycheck.

Government monopolies in certain industries, tobacco for

example, have practically nothing to do with the implementation of socialist theory. In this case the simple fact is that the government back in the 17th century was seeking additional sources of revenue and this area presented itself as a likely prospect. Similarly, the current high tax on certain kinds of alcoholic beverages is another example of trading on human desires —the morality of which cannot be legislatively determined— to fill the coffers of the state for more constructive purposes. The state's venture into still other areas of economic enterprise was not done at the insistence of socialists. Rather it can be ascertained that it was the private entrepreneurs themselves who sought socialization as a means of salvaging something from enterprises which were on the verge of bankruptcy in the 1930's. The initiative, in other words, for what can be appraised as an increase in "socialism" actually came from those who might logically be expected to be among the prime antagonists of socialism.

On taxes and their relation to increasing governmental enterprise M. Terré conceded that tax rates had gone up significantly, but he added this noteworthy comment. The tax rates, he said, were set specially high to try to take into account the seemingly incorrigible tendency of the French taxpayer to cheat on his tax returns. It may be unfortunate that this practice seems so deeply ingrained in the French personality, but this fact gives a basis for a more realistic evaluation of the tax rates as they exist. Incidentally, M. Terré suggested that the highest incidence of "modification" of income reporting and tax payments appeared to be among the professional element in the population.

Concerning any further drift to the left in French politics M. Terré offered the following opinions. While it is true that such a drift appears to be in the cards when De Gaulle passes from the scene, the drift should not be overestimated nor its consequences misconstrued. The Communists continue to exercise considerable influence—particularly through the C.G.T.—but their vote-getting capacity must be appraised in the proper light. The large segment of the agricultural population which consistently votes Communist does so in a "Poujadist" mood. It is a vote of protest not of conviction. The French farmer's individualism is simply inconsistent with the orthodoxy and regimentation of communist demands. A leftist vote therefore is simply an expression of dissatisfaction and, perhaps, one way of demonstrating a refusal to follow the lead of anyone unquestioningly. The Socialists, he confirmed, have lost the confidence of the young and may well decline further in the political scale. How much this may contribute to Communist strength remains at this point an unanswerable question.

Though a drift to the left may be expected, he concluded, one thing seems to be clear at the moment. Slogans aside, none of the left-center parties seems to be considering further nationalization of industry as the best path to greater economic recovery. As in Great Britain, the various party leaders are much more concerned with the solution to specific problems, e.g., the cost of distributing agricultural products, than they are with devising and implementing broad socio-economic programs. The greater probability is that, regardless of political leadership, the trend will be to a more widespread use of indirect controls to guide the economy. Direct participation by government will, of course, remain, but it will be secondary to the planning principle and the use of fiscal and investment policies to achieve desired objectives.

STUDY QUESTIONS AND PROJECT SUGGESTIONS

1. Discuss the social, psychological, and political aspects of French history which bear on current economic organization.
2. Indicate the reasons for the comparative decline in influence of the contemporary French Socialist party.
3. Distinguish between the two major types of economic planning in France in the post-World War II era.

4. Why is regulation of agriculture an especially difficult problem in France?

5. Compare the French labor unions (organization, orientation, objectives, tactics) with those in the United States.

6. Does the relatively high percentage of votes received by the French Communist party suggest a dedication on the part of the French people to Marxist principles?

CHAPTER 12

THE BALANCE
SHEET

Any attempt to appraise socialism as a theory or a program of action is subject to serious difficulties and most dangerous pitfalls. As has been carefully pointed out, the first difficulty arises from definition. There is no such thing as "socialism" per se; there are types, and shades, and varieties of socialism just as there are variations in architecture and values in dwellings. Secondly, there is the necessity of distinguishing between the manifestations of socialism as they appeared in different countries. Thirdly, distinctions must be made in the ramifications of socialism according to the time at which they appeared historically. And probably most important, it must be kept in mind that whenever or wherever some ideology or program has appeared bearing the appellation socialism it has tended to generate emotional turmoil either of support or antagonism which has clouded the actual content and intent of the concept making accurate assessment arduous if not impossible. This being the case, it must be understood that the following evaluation of necessity stands open to challenge on the grounds of over-generalization, prejudiced selectivity, shortsightedness, warped definition, or other bases which the critic may choose. But as was noted in the first chapter, the various types of socialists from the early utopians to the contemporary advocates do present a pattern which can be discerned. And it is on the basis of this pattern that we may make some judgments about socialism generally—its worth as a theory, its accomplishments as a platform of action, its shortcomings, or its dangers.

The first conclusion which can be drawn about socialism as a whole is that it—or something very much like it—was *inescapable*. Every society has had its imperfections, and as societies grew the imperfections normally grew with them. No matter what type of economic organization was adopted there were always those who were better off and those who were worse off. Sooner or later those at the bottom of the economic ladder have developed some plan or taken some action to remedy their plight. Violence, intrigue, argumentation, organization, appeals—all have been used at one time or another to accomplish their ends of improvement. And it has not always been the poor themselves who have taken the lead in such matters. Observers at any economic level have become discouraged or disgusted with what they saw of their societies and have set out to suggest partial remedies or theories of total renovation encompassing economic, social, and political reforms. Thus the nature of man in striving for improvement made it certain that the status quo would always be subject to examination and criticism. And the larger, more complex societies with their variety of interests competing for available economic resources were more likely to produce a succession of ideas and programs seeking change in the existing state of affairs. Socialism then is merely one of the forms of criticism which have been so prevalent throughout history and which developed in time specific economic coloration.

A second generalization which may be made is that—with some exceptions—the various socialist movements have been humanitarian, altruistic, and even Christian in orientation as the motivation for economic improvement. Material gain as such for the

masses has more frequently than not been secondary to the
idea of man's general amelioration to lead the "good life" in the
broadest sense. This is not to impute to socialism an aura of
religion which might make it more respectable in the minds of
many, but it is to note the reality of the early threads of the
movement, threads which have definitely influenced the nature
of the fabric which was ultimately produced. At the same time,
this emphasis on the "good life" should be recognized as suggest-
ing the small, independent, self-sufficient community as the ideal.
Socialism has not always sought the interference of the powerful
national state in economic affairs for the benefit of the masses.
Rather, in many instances, socialist theorists have deplored the
workings of "big government." Their communal approach to life
has envisioned a moderation of such influence or even the replacement of mammoth government by a number of smaller
societal groupings. This insistence upon ethical values as the
central theme of society's mores has continued to exercise an
influence even on modern orthodox socialism where the aims and
the programs became much more materialistic in nature and
where economic advantage—pure and simple—was sought for
one group over another. The influence has been subtle and could
be easily overlooked in the words which have described socialist
doctrine. But it has been present and has had a profound effect.

Regardless of the validity or attractiveness of socialist doctrine,
another value which may be attributed to the appearance of
socialist movements is the compulsion which it has produced in
forcing any society to examine the principles upon which it
rests and the motives which prompt its operations. In this realm
the precise content of the socialistic ideology, while not irrelevant,
is less important than the fact that it stirs thought and possibly
sets the stage for progress even if it is not along the lines which
the socialists prefer. Unless there are dire circumstances to move
them, most people seem to have a tendency to become habituated
to the status quo. They may let things slide, refuse to question,
continue in their usual routines, become lethargic, and never
think to ask themselves if this is the best they can expect of

their society. Some even become defenders of the status quo just because it has existed over a long period of time—thus becoming venerated—even though they may not be special beneficiaries of the society's economic production. Only when such a concept as socialism comes forth and is debated pro and con are they jolted even slightly out of their self-imposed apathy and their eyes opened to the questions which should be asked and to alternative answers. Simultaneously, if one notes the fervor and dedication of leading socialist theorists and practitioners there may be an additional psychological bonus. The popular apathy which is all too apparent robs the society as a whole of an enthusiasm, a vibrancy, a sense of direction which could add so much to the general happiness. Boredom, dissatisfaction, and discontent are natural results of such mental and physical laziness. But when one sees the true enthusiast in action—even though one may disagree with his cause—the fervor seems to communicate itself. There can be an identification, a vague stirring to participate, an urge to thought, at the very least a vicarious pleasure. If it can be accepted, therefore, that enthusiasm, dedication, fervor, and diligence are virtues to be cultivated, socialists—as many others—can be accepted as contributors to society's well being even if only in that sense.

In their observations about their respective societies socialists often turned their attention to the particular institutions of the society as distinguished from its broader guiding principles and the people who make up the society. In a number of cases the socialist conclusion has been that such institutions were corrupt, thus tending to absolve people from any blame. As suggested earlier, there is a certain amount of self-delusion in this because institutions do not spring into being without human calculation, and the goodness or badness of such institutions reflects as much as anything else the good or evil intent of their creators and those who sustain them. The importance of this concentration on institutions is, however, that, given the aforementioned popular apathy and the manipulative ability of a few, institutions—no matter how carefully established—may in time become something quite different. Potential institutional imperfections may not be seen at the time of establishment, and when they appear they may be minimized or overlooked. Malevolent use of an essentially good institution may go unnoticed or be tolerated through ignorance. Institutions may become overly rigid or outmoded but be retained out of respect for tradition. People may be good or bad, but even good people may have difficulty in developing and expressing their virtues in a society whose institutional practices dampen this potential. If I may resort to an analogy, the best driver in the world cannot display his skills in an automobile without gasoline, or one whose sparkplugs no longer function, or one whose steering apparatus has been consciously tampered with. In short, while people and institutions are closely interrelated, in focusing attention on institutions as well as people and principles the socialists have provided one sound criterion for societal introspection.

As regards the relationship between socialism and trade unionism several interpretations are possible either from the viewpoint of the trade unionist or of the entrepreneur. Where socialism made common cause with organized labor—as a matter of fact helped to organize it, and where trade unionists were considered major supporters of socialism and the two went forward hand in hand in program and process the cause of the unions was helped, probably to the discomfiture of the capitalists. In such circumstances—as in the United States—the more limited, point by point objectives of the unionists—higher pay, shorter hours, improved working conditions—were kept in proper perspective and were obtained a little at a time. This the organized laboring man could understand and accept. But there were two other circumstances in which the relations between the broad socialist movement and the trade union movement as such did not achieve such rapport. In one case the socialist leadership was much more concerned with broad total theories about society's renovation than it was with the picayunish objectives of minimum wage or maximum hour legislation. While the trade unionist might understand and applaud such broad aims they did little for his pocketbook or his belly, and on top of that the plans were so grandiose that they failed of achievement. Nationalization of industry, for instance, was less important to the working man than a raise in pay. The fact that many socialist leaders advocating the general theories were middle class intellectuals probably did not endear them to the workers either. The other case in which the accord between the unions and the broader movement seems to have been less than perfect was when the leadership of the socialist camp was too radical and militant, as was true of the syndicalists. Surely the syndicalists could more easily identify with the working class, and their emphasis on literal violence and sabotage probably found many adherents. But again there were things wrong. Trying to do too much too quickly led to nothing at all being done of a constructive nature. The general strike was never a truly effective weapon, and more workers than not were repulsed by the continued insistence on violence. The concept of small autonomous groupings which would develop following the overthrow of capitalism and the state was beyond the comprehension of most trade unionists; it was too novel. And the very aggressiveness of some leaders generated resistance in the capitalist camp which held the trade union movement back far longer than it should have been. Thus it may be seen that the relationship between socialism and trade unionism has been uneven—helpful in some instances, hurtful in others. If a generalization may be ventured, in the long run the union of the two contributed to the advance of both.

That socialism began as utopian theory was probably inevitable. At the times when the first observations were being made about the inadequacies of ancient or medieval societies the political, economic, and power structures of those societies were such that it was practically impossible to think that radical changes could be effected or even that the critic could be brazenly overt and blunt without risking his neck. But these utopias helped open the human mind to new vistas. As populations changed, as societies stabilized, as the industrial revolution came across the horizon, as democracy began its march, the earlier thoughts were revived to justify new pragmatic approaches to the solution of economic and social problems. The theorist became the activist; he was not always right; he could be either too cautious or too militant; he might fail to estimate properly his opposition or his following; but he was a "doer." And what it is important to remember here is that through the process of trial and error, through occasional victory and frequent defeat, the socialist advocate ultimately discovered reasonable objectives, feasible programs, legitimate processes which would effect his broader aims. This transition from utopia to empirical approach took centuries, but it may have been worth the effort.

For the moderately objective analyst reared in the democratic tradition and even influenced by the laissez-faire concept three other characteristics of socialism would have to be accepted as worthy: gradualism, constitutionalism, and compensation for private property socialized. It is redundant to note again that not all types and branches of socialism can lay claim to these characteristics. Marxism is impetuous, violent, and confiscatory. Syndicalism was hardly peaceful and democratic. Even in the more orthodox ranks occasional leaders are aggressive, in a hurry, and not too concerned with legal niceties. But if a generalization is warranted, the entire movement over the years is moderate. Some utopians, the Christian socialists, the revisionists, the Fabrians, and others have argued strenuously that the way to make haste was slowly. Even where the objectives sought were limited, a great deal of groundwork had to be laid before success could be grasped. Understanding had to be spread; confidence had to be gained; details had to be worked out; compromise may have been a necessity. All this could not be done quickly in a hostile atmosphere. Similarly, leaders like Kautsky knew that any test of violence must surely result in the defeat of the poor wherever the economic overlords possessed the preponderance of strength in an industrialized society. The strength of the masses, of the poor, was in their numbers. But it was a strength that had to express itself through that very process to which the whole society gave veneration—democracy. The way to victory was through ballots and numerical pressure on legislators and administrators, all in accord with existing constitutional provisions. The organization of the working class, the battle for the franchise, the extension of suffrage, the training of candidates—this was not a simple skirmish. It was a long hard fight, but one in which ultimate victory could be won and momentary losses not disastrous. It even implied a realization that the "class conflict" was less real than appeared and that there was an interdependence among all the members of society which could be best fulfilled by gradualistic constitutional means. No more striking example of socialist commitment to the democratic cause can be found than that described in the previous chapter on Great Britain. The fact that it occurred there may modify it as a "typical" procedure in the light of Britain's democratic traditions. But even in such an environment the spectacle of a socialist party being voted into then out of office, and de-nationalization following nationalization, can leave little doubt of the essential orthodox socialist position on legality of action. And the third theme of moderation is the matter of compensation. Here again it is repetitious to acknowledge that payment for nationalized industry has not always been acceptable to private owners as constituting the fair market value of the property. Nor can any contention be sustained that socialists individually or collectively have had or will have a tendency to generosity in such matters. For persons who have so long considered entrepreneurs as a class to be "exploiters" this would be asking too much. However, it can be claimed that socialists in theory and practice has been sufficiently cognizant of the role of the capitalist and his contribution to society and the worth of his installations that they are willing to offer at least a minimum compensation and in many cases a fairly realistic payment for that which is seized by the state.

Several other features of socialism of a relatively salutary nature remain to be examined. The first is primarily an American phenomenon previously alluded to, but particularly in view of the many misconceptions about socialism prevalent in this country it can stand reemphasis. The economic conditions of the late nineteenth century had already given rise to the organization movements in labor and farming and to the first attempts to induce government to take a hand in equalizing economic return and opportunity. Eventually this flowered into the progressive movement already described. But the progressive movement was so broad, encompassed so many facets of life, concerned itself with so many social and economic problems that it suffered a bit from a lack of focus. When the Socialist party was formed just before the end of the century and took up some of the specific aims of progressivism—along with broader socialist doctrine—a dual result was produced. In the first place, the socialist emphasis gave a new focus to the objectives especially in the area of labor benefits. This was a new force to be reckoned with and one which had a reputation for militancy and was known to reject capitalism in a way which progressivism never did. The second result stemmed from the first. Americans generally and capitalists in particular were much more willing to deal with individual problems in the context of an ideology which was native rather than an alien one which could be much more aggressive. Thus in adding focus and fear to what was already in process the socialists aided in achieving the ends of progressivism and the New Deal, though in so doing they undercut their own potential influence. If one believes, therefore, that the reforms coming from the progressive era and the New Deal were beneficial to the United States generally, socialism—American variety—must be credited with a generous assist.

Going one step farther, progressivism—New Dealism, with the possibly inadvertent help from the Socialist party, aided in preserving capitalism in the United States. Going back to the imperfection of institutions or their perversion for personal purpose, early twentieth century capitalism in America simply did not work perfectly. Monopolies, the business cycle, sweat shops, child labor, and other evils existed in a system which should have worked better for all. Assessing blame or pointing fingers is of little use now; the fact was that the flaws were there. The progressives wanted to remove the flaws; the socialists and the communists wanted to remove the system. Most Americans, including those most vociferous in their condemnation of shortcomings and misuse, preferred the former course. To the extent that American capitalism was modified then, the Socialist influence in abetting the efforts of the progressives buttressed the capitalist fortress against the onslaughts of either of the truly leftist ideologies, gained some of the limited objectives of socialism, but preserved the essential virtues of a free enterprise economy.

Finally in an estimate of those virtues, conscious or unconscious, which socialism may be said to possess is its relationship to communism. We have previously explained that the two have an ideological kinship in that they reject the basic principles of lassez-faire capitalism. Private property, the profit motive, competition and other aspects of a free enterprise system are anathema to either of these collectivist groups. But socialism is, as previously recognized, strikingly dissimilar from its relation. It is not as materialistic in origin or outlook, it is not nearly so committed to violence in its approach, it is not as total in its socializing aims, and it has more consideration for the entrepreneur. Most important, and perhaps most surprisingly, socialism has been a bitter political enemy of communism in many countries. There are several reasons for this. Conflicting personal ambitions of leaders has been one; sincere ideological difference has been another; competition for followers has been a third. Regardless of the cause, however, as each group has jockeyed for political prominence a greater animosity has developed than friendship. Neither the distinctions between these two rivals nor the rivalry itself makes either particularly palatable to proponents of capitalism. At the very least, however, some solace may be found in the fact that the more moderate, more legally inclined, more humanitarian of the two ideologies has impeded the broader acceptance of the more materialistic and more violent one.

What has been said thus far, though primarily complimentary, is not intended as a defense of or an apology for socialism. It is legitimately subject to criticism, and in action it has frequently fallen far short of its lofty aims. Faults, like virtues, can, of course, be exaggerated, but it behooves us at this point to consider as objectively as we can those fallacies and flaws of socialism which make its theory questionable and its practice hazardous.

To begin with, socialism must be recognized as constituting an attack on capitalism. With all of its humanitarianism, its gradual approach, and its concern for legality, socialism is in its modern form an economic doctrine and one diametrically opposed to laissez-faire. The significance of this position lies first in the rejection of the premises of capitalism. Any system will have its faults, but in assessing such faults one must begin with a recognition of the system's virtues—how it could or should work if the imperfections were not present. From this point of view the capitalist system has much to recommend it. It assumes what appears to be a very strong desire in man to hold privately and freely that which can reasonably be called his own property—that which he has discovered, that which he has built, that land which he has tilled. Such a desire may not be inherent in man's nature, but its continued presence in practically any society must mark it as a strong compulsion. Capitalism also assumes the value of freedom. Man should be allowed the greatest latitude in self-development, economically or otherwise, as a rational and basically virtuous being. Now freedom has its risks; the ultimate freedom possibly prescribing the law of the jungle since man is not perfect in his virtue. The strong may destroy the weak; the cunning may ensnare the unwary; security of person and property may diminish with minimizing of the restraints imposed by law and order. But with all its dangers, capitalists together with those who simply chafe under any restraint prefer greater freedom than greater security.

Additionally, the free enterprise system tends to encourage the development of virtues which are important under any circumstances—self-reliance, industriousness, initiative, ingenuity. By permitting the individual to secure private property and to utilize it to amass more through the fruits of his labor he is given an incentive to produce goods and services which will not only benefit himself but his fellow men. The profit motive, in other words, whether stated in monetary or other terms provides the urge to economic productivity, to resource utilization, to higher living standards. And so long as the freedom of competition is maintained, the entrepreneur is driven to strive more diligently for product and process improvement, thus benefiting the total society. One further point must be stressed. Whatever criticisms may be made of capitalism as an economic system, it *has produced* remarkable material gains for the populations of those states which have adopted it. It has worked pretty much as it was intended. Living standards have risen dramatically.

Now to be sure there is little difficulty in discovering capitalism's imperfections. Unfair business practices have abounded; manipulation of the system for private gain by the unscrupulous has occurred; competition has at times vanished, being replaced by monopoly; lack of concern for the mass of the working people by the capitalist has been far too prevalent; the business cycle was a reality. But given all of this, is the answer the socialists provide the proper one? Should these defects call for the elimination of the system? Are the inherent virtues not worth preserving? Is it not better to retain the system while eliminating the flaws? This it would seem is the basic criticism to be launched at socialist dogma. There is too great a readiness to condemn. There is too great an urge to surgery where medication could do the job. There is perhaps too great a sense of righteousness in propounding a panacea without a sound consideration of circumstances. Reforming zealots may be as much at fault as perverters of that which they wish to reform.

A more specific criticism levelled at socialism is that its trend of nationalizing private property and equalizing income must in time deprive individuals of incentive and deaden the initiative which is so necessary for society's advance. That from which this charge draws most sustenance is really not part of the socialist doctrine. Rather it is the Marxist dictum that when the millennium of the classless society is achieved, each person will contribute economically according to his ability, and each will receive according to his needs. From the capitalist viewpoint, the fallacy of this concept is that the more able, the more industrious, the more inventive will have no urge to exert themselves to the fullest as long as they know that the less able may receive as much or more in economic returns if their "needs" are deemed to equal or exceed those of the more capable. And judging from human nature as it may be generally observed, there appears to be strong reason to believe that such modification of effort would occur. But let us recognize that socialist doctrine does not call for the all encompassing public ownership of the communists nor for the economic leveling of all and consider the matter of initiative and incentive in those terms.

The capitalist theory, of course, presupposes the desire of all to improve their economic lot—or, to be more blunt, to make more money so as to enhance living standards and enjoy the luxuries of life. Increased monetary return is thus the incentive to work harder and be more ingenious. And in all probability most humans—especially those having been exposed to the free enterprise theory—are motivated, at least partially, in this way. But to begin with, this assumption is almost as fallacious as the Marxian concept of dialectical materialism in that it over-emphasizes the economic aspect of man's existence; dollar (or pound or franc) return is not always the primary motivation in man's endeavors. Even in the most highly capitalistic societies there have always been many who chose occupations where monetary expectations have been secondary to others. The clergy, nurses, teachers—to mention a few—generally have not followed these callings in the hope of becoming millionaires. Surely these people have sought a decent economic return, but this has been less important than other returns which they have found. Psychic satisfactions are difficult to delineate because they are so individual, but it is not difficult to discern a variety of satisfactions which might please one or another individual more than a larger bank account. The nature of the working environment, the amount of leisure time, the freedom to pursue one's interests at one's own pace without overweening supervision, the rendering of a needed service, the opportunity to train the young or care for the aged, prestige, power, influence for its own sake, the chance to be creative—all may appeal to different individuals as much or more than the opportunity to make more money in an occupation which did not have these other appeals.

There is a further flaw in the capitalist theory of incentive which enshrines material gain, and that is that its validity can be partially substantiated only in a society which accepts its basic premises. Where there is freedom to rise or fall in the economic scale and where wealth is a primary index of prestige, power, and even intellect, there will be a greater tendency to strive for that status and its symbols. But if the society is not so oriented, or if the gulf between rich and poor is not so great, does the postulate of economic incentive still hold true? Would not the pursuit of other values and other gains surpass the striving for wealth?

Even accepting the free enterprise assumption about economic incentive as the best way to human progress, must we simply rule out any hope of progress in a society in which that incentive is minimized or eliminated? What of patriotism—national or otherwise? Has not this urged man to fantastic efforts? What of honor? What of religious or ethical beliefs? What of personal, inner satisfaction for a job well done—even if not publicly recognized? And what of fear? Fear of unemployment, fear of starvation, fear of punishment have shown themselves to be powerful incentives to action. In the Soviet Union, for example, where the economic incentive along capitalist lines has been so minimized, *something* (fear, national pride, devotion to communism?) has permitted the state to make tremendous technical strides forward and even to begin to cater to the desires for creature comforts in ordinary living.

The point in examining this thesis of economic incentive is not to suggest its invalidity. This writer personally believes it has much to recommend it and that it has made a major contribution to the American society. Rather it is to suggest that there have always existed other incentives equally potent side by side with it, and that should the economic motive be removed others might supplant it. It is only in these terms that we can consider seriously how increasing socialization might affect a society's initiative. Assuming in the first place that the entire outlook of the society would be modified with the acceptance of some degree of socialist doctrine, it would seem that for the average individual there would be little change in initiative. For one thing, for those who remained in the private sector of the economy the status quo would prevail. For those in nationalized industries, initiative and industriousness would still be the pathway to the higher echelons. The innate "tinkerer" and inventor could probably be counted on to continue since the aim is generally creativity for its own sake rather than fortune. (We might note in passing that many persons now engaged in research in private industry sign away their rights to the economic fruits of their discoveries as a condition of their employment, and that, on the other hand, those in "socialized" employment, e.g., the postal service, are frequently the recipients of sizeable bonuses for money-saving suggestions.) Those who might malinger and "goof off" under socialism are, in all probability, doing so in private employment or unemployment. For the potential entrepreneur, for the occasional "go-getter" who is a mixture of fortune seeker and public benefactor, the nationalization of that economic activity which is his bent would probably have an adverse affect on his initiative. And this could be a significant loss to society, for it is not only the thinker and the inventor who help society advance, but the organizer, the developer, the salesman, the man of zest and vigor. Such characteristics are frequently intangible and only their emanations can be sensed; but let these emanations vanish and the results will be felt.

There are two senses, however, in which the validity of the indictment against socialism on the count of deadening initiative and removing incentive seems to manifest itself most strongly; one is fairly tangible, the other more nebulous. The business of government is service, not profit. Government enterprises may try to pay their own way or even show a small profit if for no other reason than to avoid the criticism of the legislature, the press,

and the public. But unlike private enterprise, the financial statement generally does not increase or decrease the amount of
money in the pockets of the directors, the managers, the supervisors, or the workers. The aim of service at reasonable rates
may require a non-profit operation. Thus there is not quite the
same kind of incentive as in private enterprise to improve
productivity, develop new processes, streamline organization, or
devise new and better techniques. And particularly during a
period of changeover, when the monetary criterion is still very
much in mind, those who might normally be counted on to be
doing these things will be less prompted to do them. The second
sense in which the criticism may be valid takes us into an area
of still greater speculation. The advent of socialism, presumably
accompanied by planning, social services, loans, subsidies, training programs, *et al.*, may well create a national environment in
which the marginally productive worker, the potential contributor to society's well being, the prospective "fireball" (with proper
inducement) may be lured into a frame of mind in which he is
more than content to "let George do it." He may come to believe
(though wrongly) that he is better off doing little or nothing
while receiving some sort of government dole though he could
receive greater income and more satisfaction even from a minimum exertion. This attitude, if sufficiently widespread and sufficiently prolonged, could induce a stagnation of effort and initiative which could prove deadly to a society.

Another frequently heard criticism of socialism, stemming in
part from the assumption of loss of incentive and directed specially at the nationalized industry, is the inefficiency of public
operation. The remarks illustrating this criticism refer to the
tardiness of public transportation, occasional power failures,
financial crises, the lackadaisical attitude of public employees,
slow mail delivery, etc. The first point to be made about this
criticism is that, in many of its ramifications, it is accurate. Most
persons have been on the receiving end of one or more services—
or lack of services—from which the generalized conclusion of
inefficiency can be drawn. And a considerable amount of propa-

ganda has been disseminated to exaggerate the fact beyond its
proper proportions. In the United States, where the civil servant
has not had the advantage of the prestige attaching to public
service in Great Britain this has been an easy task. One factor, of
course, which makes the criticism accurate is the goal of public
service at reasonable rates. Rendering the most effective service,
for example, delivering mail to outlying residences, while attempting to maintain minimum charges for the service as a whole
is not conducive to the greatest efficiency. Another is the fact
that industries nationalized have frequently been so "sick" that it
would be impossible to make them efficient except at prohibitive
cost—the coal mines in Great Britain, for instance. It is also true
that there are some public employees who take advantage of
their tenured positions to exert less than their best efforts though
they produce adequately enough to keep from being discharged
for incompetency. As a matter of fact the very size of a national
government's operations will account for a certain amount of
inefficiency—socialism or not. But here again the criticism must
be critically evaluated. Anyone who has bought and subsequently
had serviced and/or repaired an American automobile may have
some reservations about the efficiency of private enterprise. Anyone who has planned, built, or bought a house—aiming for a
target date or expecting certain modifications to be accomplished
—may not be certain of the efficiency of private enterprise. Anyone who has sought to make a particular purchase in a retail
store—let us say during the Christmas shopping season—may be
kept from damning the inefficiency only if he is reminded of
the religious significance of the occasion. Yet Christmas cards
mailed at the last moment have a remarkable facility for arriving on time. And we could go on interminably. The aim here is
not to condemn automobile manufacturers or retailers, the construction trade, department store, or any other branch of the
American economy as inefficient. The point to be recognized is
that inefficiency may well exist in either public or private enterprise and is often a result of peculiar circumstances. Similarly,
this writer's personal experience, consisting of employment in

both private and public enterprise, is that the preparation, the dedication, the ability, and the industriousness of those in public employment are every bit the equal and frequently the superior of those in private positions. Over-generalizing from individual instances is dangerous. Further, any American who has had the opportunity to travel abroad and to observe the operations of state-owned enterprises—with a minimum of national prejudice —will probably have noted that public facilities are, on the whole, no dirtier, no slower, no more inadequate, no more dangerous, no less effective than similar facilities operated privately in this country. Inefficiency of public operations is a reality and can become worse under certain circumstances. But any cherished belief that private ownership guarantees efficiency is a chimera.

Closely related to the prior charge is the caution against the dangers of bureaucratic despotism as socialism grows. Though this is not an inevitable sequitor from an increase in nationalized industries or a burgeoning of the number of governmental employees engaged in various programs, it does, perhaps, represent a danger to be considered. Governmental agencies—especially at the national level—once they have been created have a way of perpetuating themselves. It is usually not too difficult to justify the continued operation of a service agency or even of expanding its jurisdiction and personnel. Agency leaders cultivate champions in legislative bodies who may defend appropriations for the agency to the last breath. And as an agency becomes more stabilized, more secure in its position, it is quite possible for its personnel to become more careless and even callous in their relations with the public. More than this, there may be a subtle movement of agency functions from the purely administrative to the policy determining arena. In today's complex society, legislatures more and more leave the details of policy to be worked out by executives and administrators, and some of these may use the opportunity to become almost a law unto themselves. Some agencies may band together to strengthen their positions, and as the total organism grows, the potential for the corruption of power increases, with the ordinary citizen the loser. To be sure, in a society in which the amount of socialist orientation is relatively small and the democratic tradition strong, this potential for despotism is proportionately decreased. Nevertheless, the danger is not fictional even if it is not imminent.

Next in the list of charges to be examined is that of the increased level of taxation which socialism would require. Again validity and invalidity are intertwined in this matter. Presumably there would have to be some rise in tax levels to pay the interest on the bonds which had been offered in payment for nationalized industry. Funds for additional social services would similarly have to come from some tax or related source—whether it be called social insurance or not. Subsidies to agriculture or other segments of the economy would have to be financed in some fashion. Deficit financing at least for a time, might be required for public works, hydroelectric facilities, or the like. However, there is another side to this picture as well. In the first place, even in the more capitalistic societies such as the United States, tax levels reflect demands for services which have little or no relation to "socialist" leanings. The largest single item in the national budget is, of course, for national defense, and almost half of total tax revenues are dedicated to that end. Obviously there are no ideological connotations in this necessary expenditure. Another tremendously large item of expenditure is payment of the interest on the national debt whose size represents more than anything else the cost of past wars and preparedness against future conflicts. Again socialist concepts have little relevance here. Now there are many expenditures made by government which do suggest at least "progressive" if not socialist thought. The cost of agricultural subsidies, for example, is significant and accounts for a fair-sized bite out of the tax dollar. But note that agriculture is not socialized in America, and the program of agricultural assistance is motivated not only to help a depressed segment of the economy, but to permit that segment to assist others with the purchases it can make with its bolstered income. Does the presence or absence of socialism affect this portion of the tax level? The old-age and survivors insurance program is more "socialistic." Here employers and employees contribute to an insurance fund—with the national government as the custodian —out of which benefits may be derived later. This is compulsory savings through taxation, but the majority of the people seem to feel that such higher taxation is worth the benefits derived.

To return to the impact of socialism on taxation, assuming nationalized industries would still be able to pay most of their own way, it seems reasonable to believe that any slight rise in tax levels necessary to insure their operations would be compensated by lower costs for the services or products of such industries, with the profit element removed. A national health service program would of necessity require higher taxes, but the same services would have to be paid for out of individual income or premiums to private insurance firms if the national plan did not exist. Public works programs may cost money to be gained through taxes, but they provide employment and wages which find their way into all sectors of the economy and provide a broader base of taxation which may hold rates lower. In short, socialism may well lead to moderate increases in tax rates, but the modern economy is so diverse and interdependent that such increases may be unavoidable under any system—so long as citizens demand services, and in the long run the tax level may be held or even reduced. What is more important behind this criticism of increased taxation is the question of on whom does the burden of taxation fall. Should the healthy pay for the care of the sick? Should the employer care for the shortsighted, non-saving employee in his old age? Should the rich bear a heavier tax burden in comparison with the poor? These are the questions which cause the debates, and they have no certain answers.

Still another serious question about the validity of socialist claims—or those of collectivists in general—relates to the matter of social services. The collectivists have long claimed that a major shortcoming of capitalist society has been its lack of consideration for the masses, particularly when they found themselves in distress. Disparities in educational and job opportunities, inadequate medical facilities and treatment for the poor, failure to assist the unemployed, the disabled, and the aged—these are some of the charges which the collectivists have made against the capitalist system in the past. And naturally as part of their total philosophies the collectivists have insisted that, when given the chance, they would take the necessary steps to provide all those services and programs which had so long been absent. To be perfectly honest, where the collectivists have triumphed they have made serious efforts and have made significant accomplishments in these areas. Medical programs, disability benefits, unemployment compensation, pensions for the aged, and special care for mothers and children are some of the practical steps which have been taken. But two points make these accomplishments less important. The first is that the accomplishments have been neither so complete nor so perfect as the collectivists would have had us believe. In the Soviet Union, for example (though this is not strictly "socialist"), while many educational advances have been made, political orthodoxy still plays a large role in the determination of which students are selected for advanced training. Thus, one kind of barrier is replaced with another. Similarly, many social services in even partially socialized countries have not proved to be the panaceas expected and some still work haltingly. The other point is that in the less socialized countries such as the United States, programs of social service which are every bit as good if not better have been devised and implemented. The collectivists therefore stand deprived of the contention that capitalist societies are "heartless" and that only in the context of collectivist doctrine can the mass of the population be properly cared for.

There is another classical contention of collectivist theory, to which socialists by and large subscribe, which it would seem is of extremely dubious validity. This is the ideal of the formation of the classless society. To be perfectly honest, socialists—or even more extreme collectivists—did not intend to create a society in which each person was so much like every other that distinctions of ability, wealth, or motivation were practically non-existent. It has always been true, however, that collectivist ideology has emphasized a minimizing of the differences between groups and individuals so that what could legitimately be described as a classless society would exist. Seeing economic inequities as a manifestation of class divisions, it was only natural for socialists and others to advocate the elimination of the cause to obliterate the symptom. While economic competition and social stratification were somewhat realistically appraised by collectivists, the question to be raised is: "Is the ideal for which they strive as a remedy achievable?" The underlying assumption of collectivist thought is that oneness and uniformity will bring out the best in man and stifle the greed and the corruption which have so often expressd themselves in the scramble for riches. Competition, they claim, has heightened such faults and resulted in the class conflict which characterizes capitalism. Change the basic values of the system, they say, and you can change the society. But, realistically, can this be done? Will humans with all their variations be content to accept a common mold? Will they readily conform to a norm of mediocrity? In a modern, complex, industrial society, would it not be impossible to level beyond a certain point? Would not the more able, the stronger, the more intelligent naturally rise to the top, thus preserving a kind of class structure? Under any circumstances—including the communist vision of the state "withered away"—would not the economic organization of society require that some order and others obey thereby perpetuating castes, by whatever name they may be called? Is there not—perhaps innately, perhaps environmentally—a strain in man which urges him to rise, to surpass? Whatever the virtue of the "classless" society, it would appear to be more visionary than possible. And even more to the point, granting for the moment that the concept of the classless society means nothing more than improving the condition of the poor, broadening the opportunities of the masses, lessening the gulf between wealth and poverty, can it be said that collectivist societies have been more effective than those of modified capitalism in achieving this cherished goal? Can it be said that the evolving "classlessness" of the American

society is less effective than those more socialistically inclined? I
believe not.

And there is a contrary element in human nature which further undermines a corollary principle of socialist dogma. It is
the principle that the cooperative society is the answer to man's
dilemma. Classlessness is to be abetted by the common and
cooperative contribution of all members of the society—who
will then share equally in the fruits of their common toil. Human
nature is not easy to appraise over a prolonged period or in
varying circumstances. It is relatively simple to select certain
characteristics as they may be observed in specific locales or
fixed environments, but can extrapolations be made which would
hold good indefinitely? Humans can be described equally as
cooperative and competitive. But the ideal which so many socialists envisioned assumes a degree of cooperation over such an
extended period that it becomes practically unacceptable. Even
in the small idealized utopian communities conceived and
erected by socialist groups the spirit of cooperation and the
fact of cooperation deteriorated more quickly than the communities' creators imagined. Again the conflict between theory
and reality suggests the impracticality of a thesis which places
too heavy a burden on the frailty of the humans who must
translate the dream to the reality.

The actual performances of orthodox socialist parties in modern societies either as the majority grouping or as part of a
coalition regime have both stars and blemishes. Whether a particular action deserves commendation or condemnation depends
naturally on the viewpoint of the observer and analyst. The
simple fact of the matter is that socialist parties, like others,
have found themselves in positions where political expediency
and the hope of maintaining governmental influence required a
certain compromise of principles or at least an adjustment which
could be rationalized in terms of retaining a voice in policy
determination. For the completely dedicated socialist, any such
compromise might be regarded as an unforgivable defection or
defeat. For the more hard-headed pragmatist in the socialist

ranks, the necessary shift from ideological center may be assessed as a shrewd maneuver in the accomplishment of the possible. At any rate, even when in a majority position socialists have discovered that history, circumstances, and competing interests have had serious effects on their efforts to realize their program.

In this same vein, the step from any specific facet of socialist theory to its realization has always shown itself to be precarious if not impossible. The concept of centralized planning, for example, has advantages up to a point. It may very well make sense for a central planning agency to supervise the allocation of scarce resources among industries which in effect are competing for such resources as the central agency will be better able to consider the total economic picture and the needs of the whole society. Central planning may be better able to appraise those segments of the economy which need support and then recommend the tactics and financing necessary to balance the economy in a forward surge. At the same time, however, it is easy for the central planners to become divorced from the people with whom they are supposedly concerned and concentrate simply on economic factors. It is easy in these circumstances to fail to recognize the needs of regions and the distinctions which should be made in regional tactics. It can be a great temptation to move in the direction of Marxist "democratic centralism" in which ideas have difficulty in filtering from the bottom up and in which orders from the top down must be obeyed unquestioningly. The potential difficulties are perhaps best illustrated in France where the administration of many programs of social service have become regionalized in keeping with the diversity of interests the programs serve.

The concept of the communal ownership of the means of production is another dictum requiring further scrutiny. Private ownership, the socialists say, is unfair; it is the bane of economic existence; it permits the few to exploit the many. Productive facilities, therefore, should be socialized; they should be owned by all. The concept is quite attractive and may even have some rational basis, but as a practicality it is in fact an impossibility. Nationalized industries become public corporations, and the average individual has no sense of common ownership. He is not so much as a stockholder; he has no choice of managerial or productive personnel; he has no voice in policy decisions. Whatever benefit he derives, if any, from public ownership is so slight that he certainly cannot identify as being part owner of the operation. There is no consciousness on the part of the typical citizen that his lot has been improved by the transformation which occurs. Even if he is directly involved in the socialized industry his status may not change one whit. Whatever change is felt is only in the leadership level of those responsible. Thus talk of "common" ownership serves only as a rallying point for socialist support.

Still another fact of political and economic life should be noted in assessing socialist values. Socialists, as we have previously emphasized, do not seek to nationalize all economic life. They seek to socialize only those segments of economic activity which are deemed indispensable to public direction and supervision. At times they go to great lengths to specify the criteria which should be used to determine which sectors of the economy require transfer from private to public hands. All to the good. But a most consistent criterion for nationalization is the "sick" industry, one which is uneconomical, one beset by labor-management difficulties, one whose facilities are old, outmoded, or obsolete. And, for that matter, if such industries are critical in the national economic picture, socialists might be applauded for their desire to effect a rescue. The experience remains, however, that where the socialists have taken over a sick industry, they have seldom been able to nurse it back to economic health. They may not even have been able to retain the state of moderate debility to which the industry had fallen. Frankly, of course, in such circumstances it might have been necessary to expect a miracle to hope for the resuscitation of an incurably ill enterprise, and the socialists can hardly be blamed for failing to accomplish the impossible. But a blame can be assessed for any insinuation that a socialist society could produce the miracle which the leaders knew would not be forthcoming. A finger can be pointed at the suggestion that the adoption of the socialist viewpoint would create this atmosphere in which economic recovery could be achieved.

Finally, there is that criticism which is most difficult to assess, but which, if true, is the most damning indictment of socialist theory and practice. Say the critics, socialism brings with it inevitably a loss of freedom. Freedom ranks high in the scale of values of most humans, and though security is also attractive, the sacrifice of the former for the latter is frequently rejected. Of course, say the socialists, there can be no true political freedom so long as there is economic bondage, so the first step to real freedom for all may have to be the restraint of economic freedom (exploitation) for the few. Seemingly there are no absolutes in this matter, and the relative nature of freedom for a total society presents the serious problem in analysis. That socialist philosophy represents a restraint on the entrepreneur in laissez-faire capitalism is a truism, but, for that matter, so does the regulation inherent in American progressivism. Laws prohibiting unfair labor practices, trusts, monopolies, collusion and the like are restraints on the absolute economic freedom of the capitalist. Minimum wage and maximum hour legislation, laws requiring collective bargaining, laws prohibiting child labor, and similar protections for the working classes are also shackles on the entrepreneur. But are they so controlling as to debase the essential elements of the capitalist system? And, at the same time, in creating an atmosphere of more liberal return for the workers and protection for the consumer do not such laws enlarge freedom for a more numerous group while restraining it for a smaller one? Rendering value judgments on these matters is precarious at best, but the questions do suggest the inevitable fact that, in a society of competing economic interests, control of one group can be the release of another. Freedom may require restraint, especially if it be interpreted as license. At the same time the worker and the farmer too are coerced in terms of social insurance payments, various taxes, production controls, prohibition of strikes against the government, and other manifestations of a planned economy. In sum, socialist dogma of nationalized industries, a high degree of economic planning, and supervision of even the private sector of the economy does involve a reduction in total economic freedom as interpreted under capitalism. For a carefully conceived economic plan to be effective there can be little deviation with enforcement, and this of and by itself limits the choices of those who must, in any capacity, comply with the plan.

On the other hand, it would be unjust to deny to the socialist movement the contribution it has made to the economic liberation of the masses—to the opportunity for a fuller, more comfortable life through increased income and release from the drudgery of excessively long working hours and hazardous working conditions. Even where socialism has not taken root, its philosophy has been an adjunct to that particular movement which achieved these ends in any nation. In this sense, restraint and freedom are opposite sides of the same coin. Nor can it be denied that socialism's commitment to gradualism and legality must also be counted on the side of freedom. Self-restraint has come to be a hallmark of a free society, and to the extent that socialists have followed this path they have been within the tradition of freedom. Another important yardstick as to the retention or diminution of society's freedom under socialism or any other economic system is the extent to which civil and political liberties are retained regardless of the degree of economic direction imposed by government. Against this yardstick socialism scores good grades. It has emphasized cooperation and even anti-statism rather than centralized coercion. It has spread the gospel of the rights of man. It has insisted on democratic procedures. It has accepted political reverses and abided by democratic decisions. And if the United States, Great Britain, and France, with their varying degrees of "socialism" are accepted as practical examples of what can be expected, the traditionally important democratic civil rights of free speech, press, assembly, and religion are not in the least endangered by social-ist trends. The one threat which lurks far in the background is the possibility that a constantly increasing pattern of nationaliza-tion, controls, regulations, and supervision could create an en-vironment in which civil and political rights could be put in jeopardy by an unscrupulous leader determined to pervert such environment to his own ends. But such has always been the case regardless of economic system.

In the final analysis, then, we are left with an appraisal of socialism which be totally satisfactory neither to its propo-nents nor opponents. For all its ethical, humanitarian, gradual, and constitutional nature, socialism has been a disturbing ele-ment in many a society. Inadvertently, perhaps, it has incited violence. It may have created a vision of heaven on earth for many which brought frustration and distress when the vision proved to be only that. It has shown itself to be less than per-fect in its dedication to principle. It has failed to recognize some of the inner contradictions of its own dogma. It has been, as a practical political movement, the victim of either overly cautious or overly zealous leaders. It has permitted political expediency to triumph over purity of doctrine. It has at times become so enraptured by the beauty of its own righteousness that it has failed to nail down smaller but more practical gains. It at once expects too little and too much from human nature. It has been used for individual political purpose; its cause has been perverted; it has been guilty of the same sins of which it accuses capitalism. It has exaggerated. It has dedicated itself too wholeheartedly to utopianism. It may have promised too much to too many without stating frankly the cost in struggle and sacrifice which would be required for achievement.

But the picture is not exclusively bleak nor the record of accomplishment nil. The economic victory of the strong, the intelligent, the crafty, and the ingenious may be rationally de-fended, may spur on the more able, and may be in keeping with the concepts of social Darwinism. But the subordination and exploitation of the masses to the point where decent, hopeful lives become an impossibility is neither charitable nor economically sound for the whole society. The socialists sounded the call to arms against man's inhumanity to man, yet urged moderation in waging the fight to end it. They pled the cause of the common man before the court of humanity. They called for an obliteration of those practices and institutions which permitted the privileged few to live in luxury at the cost of the poverty of the mass. Yet they urged their position with reason and caution and within the limits of the law of their respective societies. Some were visionary; most were practical. "Make haste slowly," they said. "Grant the amelioration of the condition of the lowly, and all will benefit." And they achieved their goals—either through direct action on their part on in assisting movements which shared their humanitarian aims and were more palatable to particular societies. They modified the abuses of capitalism without destroying it. They contributed significantly to the rise in living standards of the average worker. And though they were frequently wrong in their ideas and their actions, and were badgered, and slandered, and fought, socialists —together with many others—succeeded in making memorable contributions to the advancement of the societies of the world.

STUDY QUESTIONS AND PROJECT SUGGESTIONS

1. Discuss the relationship between socialism and trade unionism in terms of the advantages of such relationship to both.

2. Write an essay on the theme: "A socialist society must necessarily result in a reduction of worker incentive and entreprenurial initiative."

3. Is inefficiency of operation a natural aspect of a socialized economy?

4. Describe briefly the effect of a socialist economy on levels of taxation.

5. To what extent can socialism's philosophy and practice of planning and regulation be considered compatible with political and economic freedom?

6. Summarize the advantages and disadvantages of socialism (in comparison to capitalism) as a theory and program of social and economic organization.

(The following excerpts have been selected to illustrate some of the typical ideas of socialist theorists and critics of socialism. They range from the utopians to the twentieth century socialists, and include commentaries supporting and opposing the "welfare state" as well as socialism.)

Sir Thomas More (*Utopia*)[1]

". . . Though to speak plainly my real sentiments, I must freely own, that as long as there is any property, and while money is the standard of all other things, I cannot think that a nation can be governed either justly or happily: not justly, because the best things will fall to the share of the worst men; nor happily, because all things will be divided among a few (and even these are not in all respects happy), the rest being left to be absolutely miserable. Therefore when I reflect on the wise and good constitution of the Utopians, among whom all things are so well governed, and with so few laws; where virtue hath its due reward, and yet there is such an equality, that every man lives in plenty; when I compare with them so many other nations that are still making new laws, and yet can never bring their constitution to a right regulation, where notwithstanding every one has his property; yet all the laws that they can invent have not the power either to obtain or preserve it, or even to enable men certainly to distinguish what is their own from what is another's; of which the many lawsuits that every day break out, and are eternally depending, give too plain a demonstration; when, I say, I balance all these things in my thoughts, I grow more favourable to Plato, and do not wonder that he resolved not to make any laws for such as would not submit to a community of all things: for so wise a man could not but foresee that the setting all upon a level was the only way to make a nation happy, which cannot be obtained so long as there is property: for when every man draws to himself all that he can compass, by one title or another, it must needs follow, that how plentiful soever a nation may be, yet a few dividing the wealth of it among themselves, the rest must fall into indigence. So that there will be two sorts

[1] *Ideal Commonwealths* (London: Routledge, 1887; 3rd ed.).

of people among them, who deserve that their fortunes should be interchanged; the former useless, but wicked and ravenous; and the latter, who by their constant industry serve the public more than themselves, sincere and modest men. From whence I am persuaded, that till property is taken away there can be no equitable or just distribution of things, nor can the world be happily governed: for as long as that is maintained, the greatest and the far best part of mankind will be still oppressed with a load of cares and anxieties."

Thomas Campanella (*City of the Sun*)[2]

[Excerpt from the dialogue between a Grandmaster of the Knights Hospitallers and a Genoese Sea-captain.]

"*Capt.* . . . All things are common with them, and their dispensation is by the authority of the magistrates. Arts and honours and pleasures are common, and are held in such a manner that no one can appropriate anything to himself.

They say that all private property is acquired and improved for the reason that each one of us by himself has his own home and wife and children. From this self-love springs. For when we raise a son to riches and dignities, and leave an heir to much wealth, we become either ready to grasp at the property of the state, if in any case fear should be removed from the power which belongs to riches and rank; or avaricious, crafty, and hypocritical, if any one is of slender purse, little strength, and mean ancestry. But when we have taken away self-love, there remains only love for the state.

G. M. Under such circumstances no one will be willing to labour, while he expects others to work, on the fruit of whose labours he can live, as Aristotle argues against Plato.

Capt. I do not know how to deal with that argument, but I declare to you that they burn with so great a love for their fatherland, as I could scarcely have believed possible; and indeed with much more than the histories tell us belonged to the Romans, who fell willingly for their country, inasmuch as they have to a greater extent surrendered their private property. I think truly that the friars and monks and clergy of our country, if they were not weakened by love for

[2] *Ideal Commonwealths* (London: Routledge, 1887; 3rd. ed.).

their kindred and friends, or by the ambition to rise to higher dignities, would be less fond of property, and more imbued with a spirit of charity towards all, as it was in the time of the Apostles, and is now in a great many cases.

G. M. St. Augustine may say that, but I say that among this race of men, friendship is worth nothing; since they have not the chance of conferring mutual benefits on one another.

Capt. Nay, indeed. For it is worth the trouble to see that no one can receive gifts from another. Whatever is necessary they have, they receive it from the community, and the magistrate takes care that no one receives more than he deserves. Yet nothing necessary is denied to any one."

François-Noel Babeuf (*Manifesto of the Equals*)[3]

". . . The aim of society is the happiness of all, and happiness consists in equality."

François Fourier (*Phalanstery*)[4]

"What does happiness consist of but in experiencing and satisfying an immense quantity of passions which are not harmful? That will be the fortune of men when they are delivered from the civilized, barbarous, and savage states."

Henri de Saint-Simon (*Society & Religion*)[5]

". . . In the New Christianity all morality will be derived immediately from this principle: men ought to regard each other as brothers.

[3] "Manifesto of the Equals," quoted in H. W. Laidler, *A History of Socialist Thought* (New York: Crowell, 1927).
[4] From Frank E. Manuel, *The Prophets of Paris* (Cambridge: Harvard Univ., 1962).
[5] From Richard T. Ely, *French and German Socialism* (New York: Harper, 1883).

. . . Religion must aid society in its chief purpose, which is the most rapid improvement in the lot of the poor."

Robert Owen (*An Address to the Inhabitants of New Lanark*)[6]

". . . That, then, which has been hitherto called wickedness in our fellow-men has proceeded from one of two distinct causes, or from some combination of those causes. They are what is termed bad or wicked—

First,—Because they are born with faculties and propensities which render them more liable, under the circumstances, than other men, to commit such actions as are usually denominated wicked. Or—

Second,—Because they have been placed, by birth or by other events, in particular countries; have been influenced from infancy by parents, playmates, and others; and have been surrounded by those circumstances which gradually and necessarily trained them in the habits and sentiments called wicked. Or—

Third,—They have become wicked in consequence of some particular combination of these causes."

.   .   .   .

". . . character is universally formed for, and not by, the individual.

. . . *any* habits and sentiments may be given to mankind.

. . . the affections are *not* under the control of the individual.

. . . every individual may be trained to produce far more than he can consume, while there is a sufficiency of soil left for him to cultivate.

. . . nature has provided means by which population may be at all times maintained in the proper state to give the greatest happiness to every individual, without one check of vice or misery.

. . . any community may be arranged, on a due combination of the foregoing principles, in such a manner, as not only to withdraw

[6] Robert Owen, *A New View of Society and Other Writings* (New York: E. P. Dutton, 1927; Everyman's Library). Reprinted by permission of E. P. Dutton & Co., Inc.

vice, poverty, and, in a great degree, misery, from the world, but also to place *every* individual under circumstances in which he shall enjoy more permanent happiness than can be given to *any* individual under the principles which have hitherto regulated society."

Karl Marx and Friedrich Engels (*Communist Manifesto*)[7]

"The immediate aim of the Communists is . . . : Formation of the proletariat into a class, overthrow of the bourgeois supremacy, conquest of political power by the proletariat."

.   .   .   .

". . . Communists everywhere support every revolutionary movement against the existing social and political order of things."

.   .   .   .

"The Communists . . . openly declare that their ends can be attained only by the forcible overthrow of all existing social conditions. Let the ruling classes tremble at a communist revolution. The proletarians have nothing to lose but their chains. They have a world to win.

Working men of all countries, unite!"

Karl Kautsky (*The Social Revolution*)[8]

[As regards incentives] "I am convinced that when once labor loses its repulsive character of over-work and when the hours of labor are reduced in a reasonable degree, custom alone will suffice to hold the great majority of workers in regular work in factories and mines."

---

[7] *The Communist Manifesto* (Many editions).
[8] *The Social Revolution* (Chicago: Kerr, 1902).

Eduard Bernstein (*Evolutionary Socialism*)[9]

". . . The aim of all socialist measures, even of those which appear outwardly as coercive measures, is the development and the securing of a free personality. Their more exact examination always shows that the coercion included will raise the sum total of liberty in society, and will give more freedom over a more extended area than it takes away. The legal day of a maximum number of hours' work, for example, is actually a fixing of a minimum of freedom, a prohibition to sell freedom longer than for a certain number of hours daily, and, in principle, therefore, stands on the same ground as the prohibition agreed to by all liberals against selling oneself into personal slavery."

. . . .

". . . Socialism will create no new bondage of any kind whatever. The individual is to be free, not in the metaphysical sense, as the anarchists dreamed—i.e., free from all duties towards the community —but free from every economic compulsion in his action and choice of a calling. Such freedom is only possible for all by means of organisation. In this sense one might call socialism 'organising liberalism,' for when one examines more closely the organisations that socialism wants and how it wants them, he will find that what distinguishes them above all from the feudalistic organisations, outwardly like them, is just their liberalism, their democratic constitution, their accessibility. Therefore the trade union, striving after an arrangement similar to a guild, is, in the eyes of the socialist, the product of self-defence against the tendency of capitalism to overstock the labour market; but, at the same time, just on account of its tendency towards a guild, and to the degree in which that obtains, is it an unsocialistic corporate body."

. . . .

". . . democracy is a condition of socialism to a much greater degree than is usually assumed, i.e., it is not only the means but also

[9] Eduard Bernstein, *Evolutionary Socialism* (New York: Schocken Books, 1961). Reprinted by permission of Schocken Books, Inc.

the substance. Without a certain amount of democratic institutions or traditions, the socialist doctrine of the present time would not indeed be possible. There would, indeed, be a workers' movement, but no social democracy. The modern socialist movement—and also its theoretic explanation—is actually the product of the influence of the great French Revolution and of the conceptions of right which through it gained general acceptance in the wages and labour movement. The movement itself would exist without them as, without and before them, a communism of the people was linked to primitive Christianity.

But this communism of the people was very indefinite and half mythical, and the workers' movement would lack inner cohesion without the foundation of those organisations and conceptions of law which, at least to a great part, necessarily accompany capitalist evolution. A working class politically without rights, grown up in superstition and with deficient education, will certainly revolt sometimes and join in small conspiracies, but never develop a socialist movement. It requires a certain breadth of vision and a fairly well developed consciousness of rights to make a socialist out of a workman who is accidentally a revolter. Political rights and education stand indeed everywhere in a prominent position in the socialist programme of action."

Sidney Webb (*Fabian Essays*)[10]

". . . All students of society who are abreast of their time, socialists as well as individualists, realize that important organic changes can only be (1) democratic, and thus acceptable to a majority of the people, and prepared for in the minds of all; (2) gradual, and thus causing no dislocation, however rapid may be the rate of progress; (3) not regarded as immoral by the mass of the people, and thus not subjectively demoralizing to them; and (4) . . . constitutional and peaceful. . . . The economic side of the democratic ideal is, in fact, socialism itself."

[10] *Fabian Essays in Socialism* (London: The Fabian Society, 1931).

William Clarke (*Fabian Essays*) [11]

"The answer of Socialism to the capitalist is that society can do without him, just as society now does without the slave-owner or feudal lord, both of whom were formerly regarded as necessary to the well-being and even the very existence of society."

Sydney Olivier (*Fabian Essays*) [12]

". . . Socialists would maintain that the ordering of our national life, and of the relations between individuals and social groups throughout the world in accordance with the principles of Socialism, is the effectual and indispensable process for ensuring to the mass of mankind the advantages of progress already effected and its continued and orderly development, and for the realization, in individuals and the State, of the highest morality as yet imagined by us."

Annie Besant (*Fabian Essays*) [13]

"The general stimulus to labor will be . . . the starvation which would follow the cessation of labor. . . . The next stimulus would be the appetite of the worker for the result of the communal toil, and the determination of his fellow-workers to make him take his fair share of the work of producing it. . . . The desire to excel, the joy in creative work, the longing to improve, the eagerness to win social approval, the instinct of benevolence: all . . . will serve at once as the stimulus to labor and the reward of excellence."

[11] *Fabian Essays in Socialism.*
[12] *Fabian Essays in Socialism.*
[13] *Fabian Essays in Socialism.*

George Bernard Shaw (*Socialism and Income*)[14]

". . . Socialism is an opinion as to how the income of the country should be distributed. The distribution is not a natural phenomenon: it is a matter for arrangement, subject to change like any other arrangement. . . . what we have to consider is not whether our distribution shall be altered or not, but what further changes are desirable to attain a prosperous stability. This is the closed question which re-opened in the nineteenth century under the banner of Socialism; but it is one on which everyone should try to form an original personal opinion without prompting from Socialists."

.　　.　　.　　.　　.　　.　　.　　.　　.　　.　　.　　.

". . . We endure maldistribution [of income] and even support it because it is associated with many petty personal benefits and amusements which come to us by way of charity and pageantry . . . or inheriting a fortune from an unknown relative. These pageants and prizes are apprehensible by the narrowest minds in the most ignorant classes, whereas the evils of the system are great national evils, apprehensible only by trained minds capable of public affairs. . . . We tolerate the evils of inequality of income literally through want of thought."

.　　.　　.　　.　　.　　.　　.　　.　　.　　.　　.　　.

". . . roadways and machines can produce nothing by themselves. They can only assist labor. . . . A country crammed with factories and machines, traversed in all directions by roadways, tramways and railways . . . would produce absolutely nothing at all except ruin and rust and decay if the inhabitants ceased to work. We should starve in the midst of all the triumphs of civilization. . . . Nature inexorably denies to us the possibility of living without labor or of hoarding its most vital products."

[14] George Bernard Shaw, *The Intelligent Woman's Guide to Socialism and Capitalism* (New York: Brentano's, 1934).

G. D. H. Cole (*Guild Socialism*)[15]

". . . Communist writers usually dismiss Guild Socialism as essentially a form of 'petty bourgeois' doctrine, afflicted with 'utopianism' and designed to obscure the realities of the class-struggle and to evade the necessary implications of Marxism. I can see what they mean. Guild Socialism was fundamentally an ethical and not a materialist doctrine. It set out, as against both State Socialism and what was soon to be called Communism, to assert the vital importance of individual and group liberty and the need to diffuse social responsibility among the whole people by making them as far as possible the masters of their own lives and of the conditions under which their daily work was done. Not poverty, but slavery and insecurity, the Guild Socialist urged, were the worst evils the workers needed to overcome. Freedom from the fear of unemployment, freedom at work, and the right to work under supervisors and managers of their own choosing and to rid the work-places of rulers appointed from above, whether by the capitalist employer or by the State, were the necessary foundations of industrial democracy, without which political democracy could be only a pretence. What a man was in his daily labour, that would he be in his leisure and as a citizen. 'Workers' control' must be built up from the bottom, on a foundation of workshop democracy and the 'right to work'.

It did not appear clearly until later how much the different advocates of 'workers' control' were at cross-purposes. To some of the Industrial Unionists, and subsequently to the Communists, it meant control by the workers *as a class*, to be exercised through the dictatorship of the proletariat as a whole, and was thus quite consistent with centralisation and imposed discipline provided the discipline was imposed by representatives of the class. The Guild Socialists, on the other hand, were strongly anti-authoritarian and personalistic: the 'workers' control' they stood for was, above all else, control by the

[15] G. D. H. Cole, *Socialist Thought*, Vol. III, Part I (New York: St. Martin's Press, 1956). Reprinted by permission of Macmillan & Company Ltd., and St. Martin's Press, Inc.

actual working group over the management of its own affairs within the framework of a wider control of policy formulated and executed as democratically as possible, and with the largest diffusion of responsibility and power."

John Spargo (*Applied Socialism*)[16]

"Overlooking and ignoring the central principle of Socialism, the class struggle, [critics] fail utterly to comprehend that a vast amount of private property and industrial enterprise is quite compatible with the Socialist ideal. . . . the objective of the Socialist movement is not so much the establishment of a form of economic organization as the realization of certain social relations, a state of equal opportunity in which no individual will have the power to exploit the labor and needs of other individuals."

Eugene V. Debs (*The Socialist Party's Appeal*)[17]

". . . The Socialist Party is the political expression of what is known as 'the class struggle.' This struggle is an economic fact as old as history itself, but it is only within the past generation that it has become a thoroughly conscious and well-organized political fact. As long as this struggle was confined to its economic aspect the ruling classes had nothing to fear, as, being in control of all the means and agencies of government, they were always able to use their power effectively to suppress uprisings either of chattel slaves, feudal serfs, or free-born and politically equal capitalist wage workers. But now that the struggle has definitely entered the political field it assumes for the present ruling class a new and sinister aspect. With the whole power of the state—the army, the navy, the courts, the police—in possession of the working class by virtue of its victory at the polls, the death knell of capitalist private property and wage slavery is sounded.

[16] *Applied Socialism* (New York: B. W. Huebsch, 1912).
[17] *Writings and Speeches of Eugene V. Debs* (New York: Hermitage Press, 1948).

This does not mean, however, that the workers will wrest control of government from the capitalist class simply for the purpose of continuing the class struggle on a new plane, as has been the case in all previous political revolutions when one class has superseded another in the control of government. It does not mean that the workers and capitalists will merely change places, as many poorly informed persons undoubtedly still believe. It means the inauguration of an entirely new system of industry, in which the exploitation of man by man will have no place. It means the establishment of a new economic motive for production and distribution. Instead of profit being the ruling motive of industry, as at present, all production and distribution will be for use. As a consequence, the class struggle and economic class antagonisms as we now know them will entirely disappear. Did the Socialist Party have no higher political ideal than the victory of one class over another it would not be worthy of a moment's support from any right-thinking individual. It would, indeed, be impossible for the party to gain any considerable strength or prestige. It is the great moral worth of its ideals that attracts adherents to the Socialist movement even from the ranks of the capitalist class, and holds them to their allegiance with an enthusiasm that suggests a close parallel with the early days of Christianity; and it is the mathematical certainty with which its conclusions are stated that enables the Socialist Party to expand and advance with irresistible force to the goal it has in view, in spite of the appalling opposition it has had to encounter. It is this certainty, and the moral worth of its ideals, which moved Mommsen, the venerable German historian, to say that 'this is the only great party which has a claim to political respect.' "

Eugene V. Debs (*Sound Socialist Tactics*)[18]

". . . With the sanctioning of sabotage and similar practices the Socialist Party would stand responsible for the deed of every spy or madman, the seeds of strife would be subtly sown in the ranks, mutual suspicion would be aroused, and the party would soon be torn

---

[18] Same source.

into warring factions to the despair of the betrayed workers and the delight of their triumphant masters.

If sabotage or any other artifice of direct action could be successfully employed, it would be wholly unnecessary, as better results could be accomplished without it. To the extent that the working class has power based upon class-consciousness, force is unnecessary; to the extent that power is lacking, force can only result in harm.

I am opposed to any tactics which involve stealth, secrecy, intrigue, and necessitate acts of individual violence for their execution.

The work of the Socialist movement must all be done out in the broad open light of day. Nothing can be done by stealth that can be of any advantage to it in this country.

The workers can be emancipated only by their own collective will, the power inherent in themselves as a class, and this collective will and conquering power can only be the result of education, enlightenment and self-imposed discipline.

Sound tactics are constructive, not destructive. The collective reason of the workers repels the idea of individual violence where they are free to assert themselves by lawful and peaceable means.

The American workers are law-abiding and no amount of sneering or derision will alter that fact. Direct action will never appeal to any considerable number of them while they have the ballot and the right of industrial and political organization.

Its tactics alone have prevented the growth of the Industrial Workers of the World. Its principles of industrial unionism are sound, but its tactics are not. Sabotage repels the American worker. He is ready for the industrial union, but he is opposed to the 'propaganda of the deed,' and as long as the I. W. W. adheres to its present tactics and ignores political action, or treats it with contempt by advising the workers to 'strike at the ballot box with an ax,' they will regard it as an anarchist organization, and it will never be more than a small fraction of the labor movement.

The sound education of the workers and their thorough organization, both economic and political, on the basis of the class struggle, must precede their emancipation. Without such education and organization they can make no substantial progress, and they will be robbed of the fruits of any temporary victory they may achieve, as they have been through all the centuries of the past."

Norman Thomas (*The Choice Before Us*)[19]

". . . In terms of common sense there is no case at all against the Socialist notion that the great natural resources ought to be our common possession, managed for the common use, and that the tools which require integrated operation by specialized groups . . . should not be owned by absentees who make a profit out of ownership."

.   .   .   .

". . . Redistribution of the national income should not be a process of intervention by government to restore to the robbed a small portion of what has been taken from them. It should be a process of ending exploitation and establishing a scheme of things in which production is naturally and logically for use rather than for the private profit of an owning class. . . . the immediate and essential objective of any desirable program must be the socialization and proper management of key industries."

.   .   .   .

". . . Most Socialists believe in compensation plus taxation rather than confiscation [of industries] because they believe that today we are not ready to take over at one act all the great means of production and run them smoothly, and that piecemeal confiscation of the sort which the government would likely apply invites confusion and counter revolution."

.   .   .   .

". . . An effective mandate for Socialism must be a mandate for change in the forms of government and many of the processes under which today the rule of privilege masquerades as democracy."

[19] Norman Thomas, *The Choice Before Us* (New York: Macmillan, 1934). Reprinted by permission of the author.

Norman Thomas (*Socialism Re-examined*)[20]

". . . Socialism's primary concern is with . . . the best and fairest way for men in society to satisfy their material needs and wants. . . . But it can coexist with any philosophy from existentialism or pragmatism to one of the various types of idealism, provided that it does not utterly despair of man's capacity for rationality and decent co-operation with his fellows.

The elite will not disappear even in a democratic socialist society. . . . We shall long need leaders; the problem is their selection from a broad base of well educated citizens under democratic controls.

. . . socialists . . . talk no nonsense about the superiority of private over government bigness. Great corporations have their own immoralities and enforce their own conformities rather more vigorously than democratic states."

Louis Hacker (*The New Deal*)[21]

"A revolution was started by the New Deal—not a revolution in the violent, turbulent sense, but a revolution nevertheless."

Henry S. Commager (*The New Deal*)[22]

"The roots of the New Deal . . . go deep down into our past, and . . . [are not] comprehensible except in terms of that past."

[20] Norman Thomas, *Socialism Re-examined* (New York: W. W. Norton, 1963). Reprinted by permission of W. W. Norton & Company, Inc.
[21] Louis Hacker, *The Shaping of the American Tradition* (New York: Columbia Univ., 1947).
[22] Henry S. Commager, "Twelve Years of Roosevelt," *American Mercury* 60 (April, 1945).

Barbara Wootton (*Freedom Under Planning*)[23]

". . . The whole question of the relation between freedom of enterprise and planning needs to be treated as a matter more of expediency than of principle. The traditional controversies between socialists and nonsocialists only obscure the practical issue which we have to face. These controversies are barren, first, because they are framed in terms not of quantitative differences, but of absolute systems. We have not seen, and we shall not see, the ideal socialist state: we have not seen, and we shall not see, unadulterated capitalism. Even the highly planned Russian economy, as has already been remarked, carries its fringe of private enterprise; and the Americans have their public utilities. Just as every economy in the world is a mixture of plan and no-plan, so is every economy in the world a mixture of the same ingredients—private enterprise, state and municipal enterprise, semipublic corporations, and producers and consumers co-operatives, compounded in varying proportions. Realistic discussion must concern itself, not with two extreme alternatives, but with the endless possible quantitative variations of the mixture.

The socialistic-capitalist controversy is barren, in the second place, because it involves a confusion of ends and means. The ultimate test of any economic or social policy or 'system' is its reflection in the lives of the individuals whom it affects. The values that matter are happiness, freedom, security, and the fulfillment of individual personalities in harmony, not in conflict, with one another. It is by their ability to promote such values as these that economic 'systems' must be compared: these systems are means, not ends. The assumption that happiness, freedom, security, and the harmonious fulfillment of personalities, can be realized either only where men and women are employed in the service of public authorities, or only where they are not so employed, is unsupported either by experience or by rational expectation: there is no magic virtue in public employment, no magic

---

[23] Barbara Wootton, *Freedom Under Planning* (Chapel Hill: Univ. of North Carolina, 1945). Reprinted by permission of George Allen & Unwin Ltd.

vice in the enterprise of the private business man; and the converse is equally true."

.   .   .   .

"There is nothing in the conscious planning of economic priorities which is inherently incompatible with the freedoms which mean most to the contemporary Englishman or American. Civil liberties are quite unaffected. We can, if we wish, deliberately plan so as to give the fullest possible scope for the pursuit by individuals and social groups of cultural ends which are in no way state-determined. The consumer can enjoy the pleasure of comparing prices and qualities, and spending money that is freely available to the limit of his income, just as and when he thinks fit. Industrial direction and industrial conscription are unnecessary. Planning need not even be the death-warrant of all private enterprise; and it is certainly not the passport of political dictatorship. It is true (and indeed obvious) that the *same* part of the economic pattern cannot both be deliberately planned, and left to emerge as the result of the uncoordinated actions of thousands of consumers. But consumer sovereignty, in any meaningful and defensible sense, seems to be quite unattainable and certainly never to have been attained outside the covers of an academic textbook; and there is the less cause for tears on this account, inasmuch as no ordinary consumer would be conscious whether he enjoyed that sovereignty or not. It is true also that the preservation of free choice of employment under planning would be impossible if wages were to be settled by a private tug-of-war between employers and employed, in which each party exploited its full economic strength. But against this must be set the fact that free choice of employment will never be a reality without planning, since legal freedom of choice is a mockery if economic pressure compels the chooser to accept the first available job. The right of effective choice of employment is the one great freedom which the pre-war Englishman, or American, or Continental European outside Russia, has never enjoyed. Planning could give it to him."

Ivor Thomas (*The Socialist Tragedy*)[24]

". . . The institution of private ownership in the means of production, distribution and exchange has been universally condemned by socialists, and no doubt many instances of the oppressive use of the power conferred by the ownership of property can be given. But we must ask ourselves what is the alternative, and, as we have seen, the alternative to private ownership and control is in practice state ownership and control. The possession of property undoubtedly confers power on the possessor, and that power can be, and has been abused; but the state ownership of all the means of production, distribution and exchange leads to a concentration of power immeasurably greater than the power wielded by an individual, and the possibilities of its misuse are correspondingly increased. It was possible for the Hegelian and neo-Hegelian schools of political philosophers, writing in the peace and prosperity of the nineteenth century, to represent the state as the expression of the will of the whole community, and to invest it with qualities of wisdom and goodness superior to any collection of individual citizens. But we who have lived through the Kaiser's war and Hitler's war, we who have seen the Bolshevik state and the Fascist state and the Nazi state and the Falangist state cannot entertain these metaphysical delusions. The state in practice, as we have seen, is capable of tyranny and oppression and brutality on a scale which would be impossible for a private person, and from which all except the most debased private persons would shrink. The power of the state is vastly greater than the power of the mightiest private owners of property; and men will commit cruelties and atrocities in the name of the state which they would be too ashamed to commit in their private capacity. We must be chary, therefore, of assuming that we shall cure any misuse of the power inherent in the private ownership of property by concentrating all ownership of the means of production, distribution, and exchange in the state.

[24] Ivor Thomas, *The Socialist Tragedy* (New York: Macmillan, 1951). Copyright 1951, by Ivor Thomas. Reprinted by permission of The Macmillan Company.

Ludwig von Mises (*Socialism*)[25]

". . . If a socialist community were capable of economic calculation, it could be set up without any change in men's moral character. In a socialist society different ethical standards would prevail from those of a society based on private ownership in the means of production. The temporary sacrifices demanded of the individual by society would be different. Yet it would be no more difficult to enforce the code of socialist morals than it is to enforce the code of capitalist morals, if there were any possibility of making objective computations within the socialist society. If a socialist society could ascertain separately the product of the labour or each single member of the society, his share in the social product could be calculated and his reward fixed proportionately to his productive contribution. Under such circumstances the socialist order would have no cause to fear that a comrade would fail to work with the maximum of energy for lack of any incentive to sweeten the toil of labour. Only because this condition is lacking, Socialism will have to construct for its Utopia a type of human being totally different from the race which now walks the earth, one to whom labour is not toil and pain, but joy and pleasure. Because such a calculus is out of the question, the Utopian socialist is obliged to make demands on men which are diametrically opposed to nature. This inadequacy of the human type which would cause the breakdown of Socialism, may appear to be of a moral order; on closer examination it turns out to be a question of intellect."

.   .   .   .

". . . Yet the socialist idea is nothing but a grandiose rationalization of petty resentments. Not one of its theories can withstand scientific criticism and all its deductions are ill-founded. Its conception of the capitalist economy has long been seen to be false; its plan of a future social order proves to be inwardly contradictory, and therefore impracticable. Not only would Socialism fail to make economic life more rational, it would abolish social co-operation outright. That

[25] Ludwig von Mises, *Socialism* (New Haven: Yale University Press, 1951). Reprinted by permission of Yale University Press.

it would bring justice is merely an arbitrary assertion, arising, as we can show, from resentment and the false interpretation of what takes place under Capitalism. And that historical evolution leaves us no alternative but Socialism turns out to be a prophecy which differs from the chiliastic dreams of primitive Christian sectarians only in its claim to the title 'science'.

In fact Socialism is not in the least what it pretends to be. It is not the pioneer of a better and finer world, but the spoiler of what thousands of years of civilization have created. It does not build; it destroys. For destruction is the essence of it. It produces nothing, it only consumes what the social order based on private ownership in the means of production has created. Since a socialist order of society cannot exist, unless it be as a fragment of Socialism within an economic order resting otherwise on private property, each step leading towards Socialism must exhaust itself in the destruction of what already exists.

Such a policy of destructionism means the consumption of capital. There are few who recognize this fact. Capital consumption can be detected statistically and can be conceived intellectually, but it is not obvious to everyone. To see the weakness of a policy which raised the consumption of the masses at the cost of existing capital wealth, and thus sacrifices the future to the present, and to recognize the nature of this policy, requires deeper insight than that vouchsafed to statesmen and politicians or to the massess who have put them into power. As long as the walls of the factory buildings stand, and the trains continue to run, it is supposed that all is well with the world. The increasing difficulties of maintaining the higher standard of living are ascribed to various causes, but never to the fact that a policy of capital consumption is being followed.

In the problem of the capital consumption of a destructionist society we find one of the key problems of the socialist ecomomic policy. The danger of capital consumption would be particularly great in the socialist community; the demagogue would achieve success most easily by increasing consumption per head at the cost of the formation of additional capital and to the detriment of existing capital.

It is in the nature of capitalist society that new capital is continually being formed. The greater the capital fund becomes, the higher does the marginal productivity of labour rise and the higher, therefore, are wages, absolute and relative. The progressive formation of capital is the only way to increase the quantity of goods which society can consume annually without diminishing production in the future—the only way to increase the workers' consumption without harm to future generations of workers. Therefore, it has been laid down by Liberalism that progressive capital formation is the only means by which the position of the great masses can be permanently improved. Socialism and destructionism seek to attain this end in a different way. They propose to use up capital so as to achieve present wealth at the expense of the future. The policy of Liberalism is the procedure of the prudent father who saves and builds for himself and his successors. The policy of destructionism is the policy of the spendthrift who dissipates his inheritance regardless of the future."

John T. Flynn (*The Road Ahead*)[26]

". . . In Britain the State has socialized eight great basic industries or services by taking them over under State operation. The rest of the system they have socialized under the method of economic planning. The State asserts the authority to make the plans for all forms of business—farms, factories, mines, shops. It decides on production quotas for an industry as a whole and in many cases for the individual units in the industry. It fixes the quotas and priorities on which raw materials are distributed, fixes prices at which they are bought and sold, fixes labor quotas and wages, determines who shall get credit at the banks and who shall not, and generally makes the blueprints upon which all business operations are carried on and polices those operations to ensure faithful obedience to its plans.

In short, the government takes over the general planning and direction of all industry. And in the exercise of this authority it decides which industries ought to be nationalized and operated directly by the State and which should be left in the hands of private owners to carry on under State planning and supervision. As part of this latter

[26] John T. Flynn, *The Road Ahead* (New York: Devin-Adair, 1949). Reprinted by permission of The Devin-Adair Company.

function the State, by taxation, takes the greater part of whatever profits are possible in such a system."

.   .   .   .

". . . The shallowest illusion of the workers was that socialism would end 'wage slavery.' The old Socialist visionaries like Annie Besant said, and believed, that 'laziness would disappear' when men worked for the Socialist State. But in fact the worker has now merely exchanged the old boss for a new bureaucrat. The old boss might have been a tough fellow, but he might also have been a fairly decent human being and most of them were. The boss now is a cold, impersonal being, full of theoretical humanity, far away in London and no decision can be made by any small foreman on the job without an immense amount of paper work that begins at the local office and moves snail-like through various local boards, sub-councils, regional boards and other bureaucratic nests up to London and finally back through the same succession of petty bureaus. Decisions are made by inflexible rule, with the human element extracted as, for instance, the laying off of a coal miner just a month before his pension would accrue and the bald refusal to reinstate him for the extra month to hold on to the benefit he had put in 20 years accumulating. At the annual conference of colliery managers, the chairman complained to the National Coal Board of a lack of humanity in dealing with the staffs. Short, staccato, impersonal orders in stereotyped letters have taken the place of the friendly, personal correspondence between managers and the boss. There is, he complained, 'a general atmosphere of distrust and caution in speech between one person and another which never existed before.'

Added to all this is the sinister consequence of the controls. The condition of the people in this respect is worse than during the war. Regulations and amended regulations pour from the presses daily so that neither shopkeeper nor housewife can keep up with them. If you kick you are called anti-social. If you disobey you may land in jail. There were 30,000 prosecutions for infractions of the regulations in a single year. This may be endured in war-time. In peace-time it is intolerable."

Walter Lippmann (*The Good Society*)[27]

". . . The primary factor which makes civilian planning incalculable
is the freedom of the people to spend their income. Planning is theoretically possible only if consumption is rationed. For a plan of production is a plan of consumption. If the authority is to decide what
shall be produced, it has already decided what shall be consumed. In
military planning that is precisely what takes place: the authorities
decide what the army shall consume and what of the national product
shall be left for the civilians. No economy can, therefore, be planned
for civilians unless there is such scarcity that the necessities of existence can be rationed. As productivity rises above the subsistence
level, free spending becomes possible. A planned production to meet
a free demand is a square circle.

It follows, too, that a plan of production is incompatible with voluntary labor, with freedom to choose an occupation. A plan of production is not only a plan of consumption, but a plan of how long, at
what, and where the people shall work. By no possible manipulation
of wage rates could the planners attract to the various jobs precisely
the right number of workers. Under voluntary labor, particularly with
consumption rationed and standardized, the unpleasant jobs would
be avoided and the good jobs overcrowded. Therefore the inevitable
and necessary complement of the rationing of consumption is the
conscription of labor, either by overt act of law or by driving workers
into the undesirable jobs by offering them starvation as the alternative.
This is, of course, exactly what happens in a thoroughly militarized
state.

The conscription of labor and the rationing of consumption are not
to be regarded as transitional or as accidental devices in a planned
economy. They are the very substance of it. To make a five-year plan
of what a whole nation will produce is to determine how it shall
labor and what it shall receive. It can receive only what the plan
provides. It can obtain what the plan provides only by doing the

---

[27] Walter Lippmann, *The Good Society* (Boston: Little, Brown and Company, 1937). Copyright 1936, 1937, 1943, by Walter Lippmann. Reprinted by permission of Atlantic-Little, Brown and Company.

work which the plan calls for. It must do that work or the plan is a
failure; it must accept what the plan yields in the way of goods or it
must do without."

.　　.　　.　　.　　.　　.　　.　　.　　.　　.　　.　　.

"Not only is it impossible for the people to control the plan, but,
what is more, the planners must control the people. They must be
despots who tolerate no effective challenge to their authority. Therefore civilian planning is compelled to presuppose that somehow the
despots who climb to power will be benevolent—that is to say, will
know and desire the supreme good of their subjects. This is the im-
plicit premise of all the books which recommend the establishment
of a planned economy in a civilian society. They paint an entrancing
vision of what a benevolent despotism could do. They ask—never
very clearly, to be sure—that somehow the people should surrender
the planning of their existence to 'engineers,' 'experts,' and 'tech-
nologists,' to leaders, saviors, heroes. This is the political premise of
the whole collectivist philosophy: that the dictators will be patriotic
or class-conscious, whichever term seems the more eulogistic to the
orator. It is the premise, too, of the whole philosophy of regulation
by the state, currently regarded as progressivism. Though it is dis-
guised by the illusion that a bureaucracy accountable to a majority
of voters, and susceptible to the pressure of organized minorities,
is not exercising compulsion, it is evident that the more varied and
comprehensive the regulation becomes, the more the state becomes
a despotic power as against the individual. For the fragment of control over the government which he exercises through his vote is in no
effective sense proportionate to the authority exercised over him by
the government."

Friedrich A. Hayek (*The Road to Serfdom*)[28]

". . . If the state is precisely to foresee the incidents of its actions,
it means that it can leave those affected no choice. Wherever the

[28] Friedrich A. Hayek, *The Road to Serfdom* (Chicago: University of
Chicago Press, 1944). Reprinted by permission of The University of
Chicago Press.

state can exactly foresee the effects on particular people of alternative courses of action, it is also the state which chooses between the different ends. If we want to create new opportunities open to all, to offer chances of which people can make what use they like, the precise results cannot be foreseen. General rules, genuine laws as distinguished from specific orders, must therefore be intended to operate in circumstances which cannot be foreseen in detail, and, therefore, their effect on particular ends or particular people cannot be known beforehand. It is in this sense alone that it is at all possible for the legislator to be impartial. To be impartial means to have no answer to certain questions—to the kind of questions which, if we have to decide them, we decide by tossing a coin. In a world where everything was precisely foreseen, the state could hardly do anything and remain impartial.

Where the precise effects of government policy on particular people are known, where the government aims directly at such particular effects, it cannot help knowing these effects, and therefore it cannot be impartial. It must, of necessity, take sides, impose its valuations upon people and, instead of assisting them in the advancement of their own ends, choose the ends for them. As soon as the particular effects are foreseen at the time a law is made, it ceases to be a mere instrument to be used by the people and becomes instead an instrument used by the lawgiver upon the people and for his ends. The state ceases to be a piece of utilitarian machinery intended to help individuals in the fullest development of their individual personality and becomes a 'moral' institution——where 'moral' is not used in contrast to immoral but describes an institution which imposes on its members its views on all moral questions, whether these views be moral or highly immoral. In this sense the Nazi or any other collectivist state is 'moral,' while the liberal state is not."

SELECTED BIBLIOGRAPHY

General Works

Chandler, Albert R. *The Clash of Political Ideals.* Appleton-Century, 1941.

Coker, Francis W. *Recent Political Thought.* Appleton-Century, 1934.

Crosland, C. A. R. *The Future of Socialism.* Macmillan, 1957.

Durbin, E. F. M. *The Politics of Democratic Socialism.* Routledge, 1940.

Eastman, Max. *Reflections on the Failure of Socialism.* Devin-Adair, 1955.

Engels, Friedrich. *Socialism, Utopian and Scientific.* C. H. Kerr, 1912.

Hayek, Friedrich A. *The Road to Serfdom.* University of Chicago, 1944.

Kautsky, Karl. *Social Democracy versus Communism.* Rand, 1946.

Laidler, Harry W. *A History of Socialist Thought.* Crowell, 1927.

Mises, Ludwig von. *Socialism.* Yale University, 1951.

Pigou, A. C. *Socialism versus Capitalism.* Macmillan, 1937.

Schumpeter, Joseph A. *Capitalism, Socialism, and Democracy.* Harper, 1950.

Socialist Union, *Twentieth Century Socialism.* Penguin, 1956.

Taft, Philip. *Movements for Economic Reform.* Rinehart, 1950.

Wasserman, Louis. *Modern Political Philosophies.* Blakiston, 1944.

Utopianism

Beer, Max. *Social Struggles and Socialist Forerunners.* Small, Maynard, 1925.

Bloomfield, P. *Imaginary Worlds.* Hamilton, 1932.

Buber, Martin. *Paths in Utopia.* Macmillan, 1949.

Hart, M. A. (ed.). *Utopias, Old and New.* Thomas Nelson, 1932.

Hertzler, J. O. *The History of Utopian Thought.* Macmillan, 1923.

Mannheim, Karl. *Ideology and Utopia.* Harcourt, Brace, 1936.

Mumford, Lewis. *The Story of Utopias.* Bone and Liveright, 1922.

Christian Socialism

Campbell, Reginald J. *Christianity and the Social Order*. Macmillan, 1907.

Feibleman, James. *Christianity, Communism and the Ideal Society*. Norton, 1942.

Gladden, Washington. *Christianity and Socialism*. Jennings and Graham, 1905.

Niebuhr, Reinhold. *Moral Man and Immoral Society*. Scribner's, 1932.

Nitte, F. S. *Catholic Socialism*. Macmillan, 1908.

Rauschenbusch, Walter. *Christianity and the Social Crisis*. Macmillan, 1913.

Raven, Charles E. *Christian Socialism—1848-1854*. Macmillan, 1920.

Spargo, John. *The Spiritual Significance of Modern Socialism*. Viking, 1908.

Orthodox Socialism

Bernstein, Eduard. *Evolutionary Socialism*. Schocken Books, 1961.

Dickinson, Henry D. *Economics of Socialism*. Oxford University, 1939.

Henderson, Fred. *The Case for Socialism*. Independent Labour Party, 1925.

MacDonald, J. Ramsay. *Socialism and Government*. Independent Labour Party, 1909.

Mises, Ludwig von. *Socialism, an Economic and Sociological Analysis*. Cape, 1936.

Rosenberg, Arthur. *Democracy and Socialism*. Knopf, 1939.

Fabian Socialism

Beer, Max. *History of British Socialism*. Macmillan, 1919.

Cole, G. D. H. *Fabian Socialism*. Allen and Unwin, 1943.

Cole, Margaret. *The Story of Fabian Socialism*. Stanford University, 1961.

———. (ed.) *The Webbs and Their Work*. Muller, 1949.

Crossman, R. H. S. *New Fabian Essays*. Praeger, 1952.

McBriar, A. *Fabian Socialism and English Politics*. Cambridge University, 1962.

Pease, E. R. *History of the Fabian Society*. International, 1926.
Shaw, George Bernard. *Essays in Fabian Socialism*. Constable, 1932.

Syndicalism and Guild Socialism

Carpenter, Giles. *Guild Socialism: an Historical and Critical Analysis*. Appleton-Century, 1922.
Cole, G. D. H. *Guild Socialism Restated*. Stokes, 1921.
————. *The World of Labour*. Bell, 1933.
Estey, James A. *Revolutionary Syndicalism*. King, 1913.
Field, Guy C. *Guild Socialism: a Critical Examination*. Gardner, Dorton, 1920.
Harley, John H. *Syndicalism*. Dodge, 1912.
Lewis, Arthur D. *Syndicalism and the General Strike*. Unwin, 1912.
MacDonald, J. Ramsay. *Syndicalism: a Critical Examination*. Constable, 1912.
Penty, Arthur J. *A Guildsman's Interpretation of History*. Macmillan, 1920.
Spargo, John. *Syndicalism, Industrial Unionism, and Socialism*. Viking, 1913.
Tawney, R. H. *The Acquisitive Society*. Harper, 1920.

Marxism

Berlin, Isaiah. *Karl Marx*. Oxford University, 1948.
Bober, M. M. *Karl Marx's Interpretation of History*. Harvard University, 1927.
Burns, Emile. *What Is Marxism?* Gollancz, 1939.
Cole, G. D. H. *What Marx Really Meant*. Knopf, 1934.
Crossman, Richard. *The God that Failed*. Bantam, 1952.
Hook, Sidney, *Towards the Understanding of Karl Marx*. John Day, 1931.
Hunt, R. N. Carew. *The Theory and Practice of Communism*. Macmillan, 1950.
Kautsky, Karl. *The Economic Doctrines of Karl Marx*. Macmillan, 1925.
Lenin, V. J. *Marx-Engels-Marxism*. Lawrence, 1934.
Parkes, Henry B. *Marxism, an Autopsy*. Houghton Mifflin, 1939.

Schwartz, Harry. *Russia's Soviet Economy*, 2nd ed. Prentice-Hall, 1954.

Wolfe, Bertram D. *Marx and America*. John Day, 1934.

Progressivism and the New Deal

Bellamy, Edward. *Looking Backward*. Houghton Mifflin, 1898.

Croly, Herbert. *Progressive Democracy*. Macmillan, 1914.

George, Henry. *Progress and Poverty*. Schalkenbach Foundation, 1956.

Hacker, Louis M. *The Shaping of the American Tradition*. Columbia Univ., 1947.

Lloyd, Henry D. *Wealth against Commonwealth*. Harper, 1894.

Rauch, Basil. *The History of the New Deal 1933-1938*. Creative Age, 1944.

Roosevelt, Theodore. *The Works of Theodore Roosevelt*. Scribner's, 1926.

Rosenman, Samuel I. (ed.) *The Public Papers and Addresses of Franklin D. Roosevelt*. Random House, 1938; Macmillan, 1941.

Rozwenc, Edwin C. (ed.) *The New Deal*. D. C. Heath, 1949.

Veblen, Thorstein. *The Theory of the Leisure Class*. Macmillan, 1899.

Wilson, Woodrow. *The New Freedom*. Macmillan, 1913.

British, French, and American Socialism

Attlee, Clement R. *As It Happened*. Viking, 1954.

Baum, Warren C. *The French Economy and the State*. Princeton University, 1958.

Debs, Eugene V. *Writings and Speeches of Eugene V. Debs*. Hermitage, 1948.

Egbert, Donald D. and Stow Persons. (eds.) *Socialism and American Life*. Princeton University, 1952.

Gaitskell, Hugh. *Socialism and Nationalization*. Fabian Society, 1956.

Hillquit, Morris. *Socialism in Theory and Practice*. Macmillan, 1912.

Jay, Douglas. *Socialism in the New Society*. Longmans, 1962.

Jeanneney, Jean-Marcel. *Forces et Faiblesses de l'Economie Française*. Paris, 1956.

Kipnis, Ira. *The American Socialist Movement*. Columbia University, 1952.

McKenzie, Norman. (ed.) *Conviction*. McGibbon and Kee, 1958.

Seidler, Murray B. *Norman Thomas: Respectable Rebel.* Syracuse Univ., 1961.

Sweezy, Paul M. *Socialism.* McGraw-Hill, 1949.

Thomas, Norman. *The Choice Before Us.* Macmillan, 1934.

————. *Socialism Re-examined.* Norton, 1963.

INDEX

236

NOTES

NOTES

NOTES

NOTES

NOTES

NOTES

NOTES

NOTES